# Pilgrim's Guide to Rome

# to Rome

### MICHAEL WALSH

CANTERBURY
PRESS
Norwich

© Michael Walsh 2015

First published in 2015 by the Canterbury Press Norwich
Editorial office
3rd Floor, Invicta House,
108–114 Golden Lane,
London EC1Y OTG, UK

Canterbury Press is an imprint of Hymns Ancient &
Modern Ltd (a registered charity)
13A Hellesdon Park Road, Norwich,
Norfolk NR6 5DR, UK

www.canterburypress.co.uk

British Library Cataloguing in Publication data

A catalogue record for this book is available
from the British Library

978 1 84825 618 7

Typeset by Regent Typesetting, London
Printed and bound in Great Britain by
CPI Group (UK) Ltd, Croydon, CRO 4YY

# Contents

# List of Illustrations

The publisher acknowledges with thanks permission to use copyright owners' photographs. Every effort has been made to locate the sources, and names of photographers are included where available. We would be grateful to be informed of any omissions. Wikimedia Commons images are used by a Creative Commons Attribution-ShareAlike 3.0 licence.

# LIST OF ILLUSTRATIONS

14 Santa Maria della Vittoria: Bernini's ecstasy of St Teresa of Avila. Photo by Nina-no.
   http://commons.wikimedia.org/wiki/Santa_Maria_della_Vittoria#/media/
   File:Santa_Maria_della_Vittoria_-_4.jpg
15 Santa Prassede: the apse.
   http://upload.wikimedia.org/wikipedia/commons/d/d9/
   Apsis_mosaic_S_Prassede_Rome_W1.jpg
16 Catacomb of Priscilla: earliest Madonna and Child?
   http://upload.wikimedia.org/wikipedia/commons/e/e2/Madonna_catacomb.jpg

## Pages

35 San Pietro in Vaticano. Photo by Mstyslav Chernov.
   http://commons.wikimedia.org/wiki/File:St._Peter%27s_Basilica_view_from_
   Saint_Peter%27s_Square,_Vatican_City,_Rome,_Italy.jpg
39 San Giovanni in Laterano. Photo be Jastrow.
   http://commons.wikimedia.org/wiki/File:Facade_San_Giovanni_in_Laterano_
   2006-09-07.jpg
43 Santa Maria Maggiore. Photo by MarkusMark.
   http://commons.wikimedia.org/wiki/File:263SMariaMaggiore.jpg
44 Santa Maria Maggiore: reliquary of the manger. Photo by Jastrow.
   http://commons.wikimedia.org/wiki/Basilica_di_Santa_Maria_Maggiore_
   (Rome)#/media/File:Sacra_culla_SM_Maggiore.jpg
46 San Paolo fuori le Mura. Photo by Berthold Werner.
   http://commons.wikimedia.org/wiki/Basilica_di_San_Paolo_Fuori_le_Mura#/
   media/File:Roma_San_Paolo_fuori_le_mura_BW_1.jpg
47 San Paolo fuori le Mura: interior. Photo by Tango7174.
   http://commons.wikimedia.org/wiki/Basilica_di_San_Paolo_Fuori_le_Mura#/
   media/File:Lazio_Roma_SPaolo1_tango7174.jpg
55 Sant' Agostino: tomb of St Monica. Photo by Isaia da Pisa.
   http://en.wikipedia.org/wiki/Saint_Monica#mediaviewer/File:MonicaSAgostino.
   jpg
57 Sant'Alfonso de'Liguori all'Esquilino.
   http://upload.wikimedia.org/wikipedia/commons/1/1b/Chiesa_di_
   Sant%27Alfonso_all%27Esquilino_Roma.jpg
61 Sant' Andrea al Quirinale: Monument to St Stanislaus Kostka. Photo by Torvindus.
   http://en.wikipedia.org/wiki/Stanislaus_Kostka#mediaviewer/
   File:SStanislausKostka01.jpg
63 Sant' Andrea della Valle.
   http://upload.wikimedia.org/wikipedia/commons/9/9z/Sant_Andrea_della_Valle_
   Roma.jpg?uselang=en-gb
75 San Carlo al Corso: reliquary of the heart of Charles Borromeo. Photo by SteO153.
   http://commons.wikimedia.org/wiki/San_Carlo_al_Corso_(Rome)#/media/
   File:SanCarloCorso-CuoreSCarlo01-SteO153.jpg
79 Chiesa Nuova: tomb of Philip Neri.
   http://en.wikipedia.org/wiki/Philip_Neri#mediaviewer/File:S_Filipo_Neri_chapel.
   jpg
81 San Clemente: interior.
   http://commons.wikimedia.org/wiki/San_Clemente_(Rome)#/media/File:Interior_
   of_San_Clemente,_Rome.jpg
82 San Clemente. Photo by MarkusMark.
   http://commons.wikimedia.org/wiki/San_Clemente_(Rome)#/media/
   File:260SClemente.jpg

# LIST OF ILLUSTRATIONS

# LIST OF ILLUSTRATIONS

# Preface

Rome is one of the world's most enthralling cities, and it has the great advantage of being comparatively small. The eager pilgrim can walk from St Peter's basilica where St Peter, the first in the long list of popes, is thought to be buried, across the Tiber to the Colosseum where many believe early Christians to have been thrown to the lions (they probably weren't, at least not in the Colosseum) in about an hour and a half. Such a walk would begin on the Via della Conciliazione, constructed to mark the 1929 accords between the Kingdom of Italy and the Holy See, the collections of treaties, known as the Lateran Pacts, which, among other things, established the Vatican City State. This broad thoroughfare was driven through the maze of narrow streets that once constituted the 'Borgo', a word derived from the Anglo-Saxon 'burg' or borough. It was in the Borgo that King Ine of Wessex – who abdicated in 726 and, like his predecessor King Caedwalla, journeyed to Rome to die – built the Schola Saxonum, a hospice for English pilgrims. It eventually became the Hospital of the Holy Spirit, and the nearby church, Santo Spirito in Sassia, recalls in its name the area's Saxon origins.

After crossing the river, the walk to the Colosseum will pass not far from the Venerable English College, a distant descendant of the Schola Saxonum, where students from England are trained for the Catholic priesthood. Nearby is the Cancelleria, the first of the great Renaissance palaces where in the late eighteenth century Henry, Cardinal Duke of York, had an apartment. He lent it to the estranged wife of his brother Charles, Bonnie Prince Charlie, until he discovered she was having an affair with a poet and threw her out. Anyone walking this route is now passing close to the Campo dei Fiori. There a statue of Giordano Bruno marks the spot where this Dominican friar was put to death for heresy – in London for a few years as part of the entourage of the French ambassador, he was a spy reporting to the government of Elizabeth I on the doings of his English co-religionists.

Later on the route goes alongside the Gesù, the magnificent church which once served as the headquarters of the Society of Jesus and became the architectural model for Jesuit churches throughout the world – except in Britain, where Jesuits appear to have gone, architecturally, straight from sixteenth-century priests' holes to nineteenth-century neo-Gothic. The Jesuit Superior General, the 'Black Pope' as he is sometimes known, no longer lives there. He has since moved his office much closer to the Vatican, to the Borgo Santo Spirito. Carrying on towards the Colosseum through the Piazza Venezia, no one can avoid seeing the monument to Vittorio Emanuele II, the king whose army in 1870 wrested Rome from papal control and established it as the capital of a united Italy. According to one account, it was British troops in Rome during World War II who dubbed this enormous monument, all too visible from many parts of the city, 'the wedding cake'. The nickname has stuck.

Any guide to Rome, and there are many of them, will list all these sights and much, much else. They will also quite probably organize the sights to be seen in a series of walks around the city. But this book is not a tourist guide. I have presumed that those coming to Rome out of devotion will have particular churches they wish to visit, shrines at which they want to pray, and I have tried to lay out information about such places as schematically as possible for easy reference. So although an annotated list of guidebooks has been included, this small volume is concerned only with those places in the eternal city to which people might come on pilgrimage.

It is true that, in Rome, there is an inextricable mingling of sacred and secular. To me, San Clemente is one of the most atmospheric of all Roman churches, not only because of its simple beauty but also because its name stretches back to the very first years of Christianity in the city. Yet even that has its pagan past. Deep beneath it, and accessible to visitors, is an early Christian basilica but below that again runs a Roman street beside which stands an altar dedicated to the god Mithras, a favourite deity of Roman legionaries, and the remains of a 'school' where the Mithraic mysteries were taught to initiates. Perhaps even more extraordinary, as will be explained in the text, is the basilica of Santi Giovanni e Paolo beneath which two Roman houses have been discovered.

These houses are well worth a visit, but such archaeological sites of pagan Rome are not the focus. There are more than enough churches – there are said to be nine hundred in all – and shrines in Rome to occupy the allotted number of pages if the book is to remain small enough to fit into a jacket pocket or slip into a handbag. But it is undoubtedly a book about Rome, and in Rome, of course, though many languages may be heard, the *lingua franca* is inevitably Italian. A list of common Italian words and phrases has been included, but rather more problematic are the names of churches. It would be a bit odd to keep referring to St Peter's as the 'basilica di San Pietro', or the Lateran basilica as 'San Giovanni in Laterano'. On the other hand no English-speaker I have ever met in Rome talks about St Clement's when they mean San Clemente, or, indeed, St John and St Paul rather than Santi Giovanni e Paolo. And 'Santa Maria sopra Minerva' is in any case pretty well untranslatable. I have therefore employed for preference the Italian name (though indicating the English version). Finally, I have already written the word 'basilica' several times. It is explained in the Glossary. May I suggest that those reading this book look at this short list of terms before launching into the text proper? It will make life easier.

# PART I

# I

# Rome: A (Very) Brief History

The foundation myth of Rome is the story of Romulus and Remus, the twin brothers abandoned at birth and reared by a she-wolf, as famously depicted in a sculpture on the Capitoline Hill, overlooking the ancient Forum. The date is traditionally 753 BC, and subsequent dates were worked out from this, so Christ was born 753 years after the foundation of the city, AUC or Ab Urbe Condita. (The fact that this date for Christ's birth is almost certainly wrong is another story – but it is not far out.) 'Urbs', incidentally, means 'city': ancient Romans regularly referred to their home town simply as the 'urbs': for them it was THE city. Again according to the foundation myth, Romulus and Remus could not agree on exactly where to build: there was a falling out, Remus was killed and Romulus named the new settlement after himself. At first it was governed by kings, but around 500 BC the last king was driven out and a republic established. It was highly successful. Rome's power extended far beyond Italy, even to Britain, but its military might brought to the fore two great generals, Gnaeus Pompeius Magnus, or Pompey the Great, and Julius Caesar. There was a civil war between the two factions in which Caesar triumphed. Caesar was now by far the most powerful man in Rome, and many feared he would declare himself king. In March 44 BC he was assassinated in the Senate House. In the turmoil which followed, his adopted son Octavian emerged triumphant. He took the title 'imperator' by which Roman soldiers hailed a successful general, and in 27 BC the Senate bestowed on him the title of 'Augustus', which became the name by which he has since been known. The 'Empire' was born.

Much has been written about 'the decline and fall of the Roman Empire'. It is important to remember that the Empire was not the same thing as Rome. Towards the end of the third century a separate structure was established to govern the eastern part of Rome's dominions and in AD 330 the Christian Emperor Constantine created a new city of Constantinople on the site of what had been the Greek city of Byzantium. With the incursion of German tribes into the western part of the Empire from the fourth century onwards, Rome, and Italy, fell out of the control of Constantinople, the last western Roman Emperor, Romulus Augustulus, being deposed in 476 by Odoacer, a 'barbarian' general. (His exact ethnicity is unclear.)

It was at this period that the papacy emerged as a significant force in Italy. They had to look after the (much diminished) population of Rome and to do so acquired estates which they managed for the good of the city. Though they might acknowledge the sovereignty of the Emperor in Constantinople, they were the effective governors of the city, even if, to retain control of their lands, the Papal States, they had from time to time to depend on the rulers of what we would now call France – Pope Leo III crowned Charlemagne as Emperor in the West on Christmas Day 800 – or later of Germany. These challenges were usually from external forces, the Normans among them or Muslims from North Africa who were known as Saracens, but often enough the people of Rome themselves proved unruly, sometimes the papal militia, sometimes the Roman nobility. In the twelfth century there was an attempt to restore what was remembered of the constitution of Republican Rome, but the papacy, although making concessions to allow civil government to be in the hands of the people, regained the ascendancy. The truth was that the economy of Rome needed the papacy, as was demonstrated in the period from 1309 to 1377 when successive popes lived in Avignon and then again during the disputed papacy from 1378 to 1415 when there were two, and for a time three, rival claimants. Rome suffered badly from the loss of revenue usually brought into the city by pilgrims.

When the popes came back, Rome once again flourished, particularly so in the two centuries from around 1450 to 1650. It became a haven for artists, for painters, sculptors, musicians and for men of letters. New churches were built, such as St Peter's, and ancient ones ornamented to the baroque taste of the day. Popes interested themselves – or at least some of them did – not just in the beautification of their own apartments but in the town planning of the whole city. And not just the popes. Cardinals likewise, most of them from noble and wealthy families, spent money putting up magnificent palaces. The only hiatus in this papal project came in May 1527 when the army of the Emperor Charles V and a band of Lutherans determined to bring down the antichrist who was the pope sacked the city, slaughtering perhaps as many as twelve thousand of its inhabitants and rendering much of it uninhabitable.

For much of their income the popes relied on the Papal States, badly managed though they were for the most part – there were sporadic attempts to improve the administration which was in the hands of clerics. But then in 1796 Italy was invaded by Napoleon's armies. The Papal States disappeared and Rome was declared a republic. First Pius VI then Pius VII were imprisoned by the French, who looted as many of the portable works of art as they could and carried them off to Paris. After the collapse of Napoleon's empire the papacy – and many of the artworks – came back to Rome, and the Papal States were restored. But the seeds of independence had been sown. Gradually the States fell to the armies of the new Kingdom of Italy until only Rome itself was left. This was captured in 1870 and the Pope, Pius IX, declared himself a prisoner in the Vatican, refusing to accept the terms the government of Italy was offering. The impasse lasted until 1929 when Italy and the Vatican (or more correctly the Holy See) signed the Lateran Pacts, a series of agreements on (1) the establishment of the Vatican City as a sovereign state; (2) compensation for the Holy See's loss of revenue – a considerable sum; and (3) a 'concordat' regulating relations between the Holy See and Italy on religious issues. The Lateran Pacts were marked by the building of the Via della Conciliazione, leading down from the piazza in front of St Peter's to the Tiber.

The role of the Pope – Pius XII – during World War II is controversial, but here we are concerned with Rome not with the papacy. Pius wanted it to be declared an 'open city' because of the treasures which lay within it, but from the Allied perspective it was in the hands of the enemy, first of the Italians and then, when Italy surrendered to the Allies, of the Germans. There was some bombing of strategic targets, the marshalling yards for instance, but in one raid a single plane dropped a bomb on the Vatican causing a little damage, and in another major attack the basilica of San Lorenzo fuori le Mura was very badly damaged and many civilians were killed. It was a pointless target in itself, but it was – and is – very close to Termini, Rome's main railway station. In comparison to many other cities of warring Europe, however, Rome emerged from the war relatively unscathed.

Before the war Italy's leader 'Il Duce', Benito Mussolini, had attempted to revive the city's imperial past. As one walks down the aptly named Via dei Fori Imperiali from the Piazza Venezia towards the Colosseum, on a wall to the right there is an image of Rome's former empire. A more common reminder of the city's glory days, however, can be found in many places but perhaps most obviously on manhole covers, the letters SPQR. In Latin, it stands for 'Senatus Populusque Romanus': 'The Senate and People of Rome'.

# 2

# Pilgrimage to Rome

The Venerable Bede, the only English-born Doctor of the Church, was writing his *History of the English Church and People* in his monastery in Northumbria during the last decades of his life – he died in 735 at the age, probably, of sixty or sixty-one. He almost certainly never left Northumbria himself but he knew, and knew of, plenty of people who had travelled to Rome including Benedict Biscop, who had founded Bede's monastery and had made the journey no fewer than six times. Bede wrote this of two successive kings of Wessex who were more or less his contemporaries:

> On Cadwalla's departure for Rome, he was succeeded as King by Ine, who was of the blood royal. Having ruled the nation for thirty-seven years, Ine abdicated and handed over the government to younger men. He then set out to visit the shrines of the Apostles during the pontificate of Gregory [II], wishing to spend some of the time of his earthly pilgrimage in the vicinity of the holy places, hoping thereby to merit a warmer welcome from the saints in heaven. (Bk 5, chapter 7)

Bede goes on to say that many English people did likewise, including King Offa, of Offa's Dyke. Obviously not everyone who set out on pilgrimage to Rome intended to die there, but all hoped to gain merit by being in proximity to the Apostles and to the relics of the martyrs.

Not, of course, that Rome was the chief place of pilgrimage. The holiest sites were those where Christ had lived and died. In the early 380s a Galician woman called Egeria had visited the Holy Land and wrote a long description of her journey in a letter to women friends back home. Fifty years earlier Helena, the mother of the Emperor Constantine, had made a similar journey and, though she left no account of it, she brought back what was believed to be the cross on which Christ had died (see **Santa Croce in Gerusalemme**): Evelyn Waugh wrote an entertaining novella based – very loosely – on her life.

Nonetheless Rome and its tombs, whether of Peter and Paul or of other martyrs, were a prime target for the devout. There are graffiti of the sort 'I was here' to be found in the catacombs showing that they had been visited from the very earliest times, even before the so-called 'Peace of the Church' marked by the Edict of Milan of 313 – though whether this was a formal edict is doubtful. What is more remarkable is that pilgrimage to Rome continued even though the journey was hazardous. When Benedict Biscop, Cadwalla and Ine went, for instance, much of Italy was in turmoil thanks in part to barbarian invasions or the efforts of Emperors in Constantinople to assert their authority. It is true that the number of visitors varied, especially perhaps after another tomb of an apostle, that of St James in the city now named after him, Santiago de Compostela, became an alternative attraction, and possibly rather easier to reach. A guidebook on how to get there was produced, known now as the *Codex Calixtinus* after the Pope for whom it was supposedly composed, Callistus (or Callixtus) II (1119–24), though scholars think it was written rather later, about 1150.

There survives a guidebook to Rome written in the form of walks – or itineraries – around the city produced sometime in the ninth century and now to be found in the monastery of Einsiedeln in Switzerland. At around the same time as the *Codex Calixtinus* was being produced, there appeared a book entitled *Mirabilia Urbis Romae*, 'The Marvels of Rome', compiled by a canon of St Peter's basilica called Benedict. It is tempting to see this renewed interest in pilgrimage and in the city of Rome as a consequence of the doctrine of indulgences, but that would be anachronistic; in any case, the *Mirabilia* is as concerned with the secular monuments of Rome as it is with the religious ones. It perhaps reflects the return to classical studies because of what historians call the Twelfth-Century Renaissance, but what it undoubtedly reflects is the increasing interest in Rome of both pilgrims and general sightseers. People had to come to Rome for all sorts of reasons, and a guide to the traditions of the city would be a welcome addition to their luggage: the *Mirabilia* circulated in many manuscripts for several centuries.

But what it was not was a book of instructions on how to reach the city. In that it differed markedly from the *Codex Calixtinus*, to which there was nothing similar for the Via Francigena. The Via Francigena was the name given to the route down through France to Italy and on to Rome taken by pilgrims to the eternal city – but also often enough by pilgrims whose final destination was the Holy Land and for whom Rome was only a stopping-off point. It was an established itinerary by the middle of the ninth century when it was first named, and in the twentieth century it was declared by the Council of Europe 'a European cultural route': ten years after that, in 2004, it was declared 'a *major* European cultural route'. It has not changed very much. Around 990 Sigeric the Serious, Archbishop of Canterbury from the previous year, made the journey to Rome along the Via Francigena to collect his pallium, the stole bestowed by the pope on metropolitan archbishops to mark their union with the See of Rome. One of his entourage described in considerable detail not the journey there but the journey back to Canterbury, and all their stopping places. Obviously place names have changed, but Sigeric's route can still be traced.

Though the gaining of indulgences was not the motive of pilgrims to Rome in the early Middle Ages, as the doctrine of indulgences developed it became a powerful factor. Pope Boniface VIII declared 1300 to be a year of Jubilee, or Holy Year, a time of special remission of debts. Crowds flocked to the eternal city in huge numbers, estimated to have been some 20,000, to obtain not just pardon for their sins, but having confessed them and having visited the basilicas of St Peter and of St Paul every day for 15 days, they would be granted complete remission of their punishment in Purgatory. This was too great a benefit to the souls of the faithful to be limited to once every century. There was a Holy Year every 50 years and, in modern times, every 25 years. Even though belief in indulgences, which took a serious knock at the Reformation, is in steep decline even among Roman Catholics, pilgrim numbers during Holy Year still remain high, no doubt to the benefit of their souls but also to the economic viability of Rome.

# 3

# Getting There and Getting Around

Medieval pilgrims had no alternative. If they wanted to visit Rome they had to walk – or, were they wealthy enough, to ride. These days, of course, one can fly or travel by train but some still choose to walk. Though there are a number of accounts written relatively recently, the classic narrative of travelling on foot is Hilaire Belloc's *The Path to Rome*, first published in 1902 and still in print. It is well worth reading. Inspired perhaps by the immense, and growing, popularity of the *Camino*, the pilgrim route to Santiago de Compostela, the number of pilgrims walking to Rome, usually – in the UK – from Canterbury in the manner of Sigeric the Serious, has been growing. Like the Confraternity of St James, which promotes the *Camino* and provides services for pilgrims (www.csj.org.uk: there are comparable organizations in many other countries), Britain now has a Confraternity of Pilgrims to Rome (www.pilgrimstorome.org.uk). This organization will issue the 'credential' – a term taken from the *Camino* – or pilgrim's passport which has to be stamped daily while en route. In Santiago the pilgrim office issues a 'Compostela', a certificate of having completed the journey – on foot, by bicycle or even, though this is rarer these days, on horseback. There is a similar arrangement for those arriving in Rome with their credential duly stamped: similar, but not the same. It is again allotted to those travelling by foot, by bicycle or by horse, but there are two different types of the 'Testimonium', as the certificate given out in Rome is called. To understand these, consult the website of the Confraternity of Pilgrims to Rome. It should be made clear to devout RCs that neither the Compostela distributed in Santiago, nor the Testimonium handed out in Rome, is an indulgence!

For obvious reasons, walkers and cyclists are relatively few. More, and especially large groups of pilgrims, will arrive in Rome's Termini station by train direct from Paris and leave the same way. Most visitors will travel by plane. There are two airports serving Rome, Fiumicino and Ciampino. Fiumicino is further away, but there is a speedy train service into Stazione Termini and tickets can easily be purchased from machines on the station. Ciampino is rather more complicated. There is a train service, but it is necessary to take a bus to the station. There is also a bus which takes passengers to a stop on Rome's Metro. On the other hand both airports are served by the Terravision bus, a service which also operates in England. Fares are cheap, the bus journey into Termini does not last much longer than by other forms of transportation, and tickets can be booked in Britain at a modest discount via the website: www.terravision.eu.

Termini is a convenient place to arrive. There are, of course, taxis available just outside but it is also the station on the Metro where its two lines coincide. The Metro, limited though it be, is a good way to get around even though the station closest to the Vatican, Ottaviano on Linea A, is a good seven or eight minutes' walk away from St Peter's: it is difficult to get lost alighting there – just follow the crowd! Tickets, which have a flat rate wherever you are travelling within Rome, are the same for the Metro or the buses or, for that matter, on the trams that run through Trastevere. They can be bought at machines on Metro stations, at tobacconists, in some bars and at newspaper kiosks. It is possible to buy day, three-day and weekly tickets. Transport is run by ATAC which has a not very helpful website (www.atac.roma.it) mainly in Italian, and while it appears to offer an English translation, it doesn't really do so. ATAC has an information office in front of Termini where one can buy a useful map of Rome's bus lines and other transport links. As in some other cities on the continent of Europe tickets on the buses last for 75 minutes: that is to say, a passenger can travel on as many buses as he or she wishes for that period of time on the same ticket. On the Metro, however, a ticket can only be used once, from entering the station to leaving at one's destination. On the buses, passengers have to 'validate' a ticket the first time it is used by putting it into a machine on the bus. This stamps the date and time. It only has to be done once, no matter how many journeys are made within the time allowed. The same is true, incidentally, for tickets for train journeys: they have to be validated on station platforms, and failure to do so can result in a fine.

A note about taxis. Licensed ones will be emblazoned SPQR and they will be metered. Within the city be careful to take one of these. Similarly, take a licensed taxi from the airport. This is a good option if there are several (no more than four) of you, because the price is fixed.

Finally, it is worth paying a visit to the office of Opera Romana Pellegrinaggi (www.operaromanapellegrinaggi. org). It is described on its website as 'an activity of the Vicariate of Rome, Department of the Holy See, at the direct dependence of the Cardinal Vicariate of the Holy Father' and its remit includes not just Rome but many other shrines in Italy and elsewhere. In Rome itself it organizes tours of the main Christian sites, and runs an open 'hop-on, hop-off' bus around the city. It also sells an 'Omnia' card, a three-day pass to the main Vatican museums and sites (with a discount at others), access to the bus just mentioned, and free travel on Rome's buses and Metro system as well as some other benefits. It is a good way to ensure that you do not miss the major sights of the eternal city, but it is not a cheap option. The Opera Romana Pellegrinaggi has three offices, but the easiest one to find is that in the bottom left-hand corner of the piazza just before entering the piazza in front of St Peter's, at Piazza Pio XII 9 (Piazza San Pietro). The phone number for this service is (+39 06698961) and the email address is info@operaromanapellegrinaggi.org. The offices are open from 9.00 to 18.00, with no break for lunch at the office in Piazza Pio XII.

# 4

# Rome: A Survival Guide

## Eating

There are many places to eat in Rome, as there are in most big cities, and at very many of them it is possible to lunch or dine outside, which is not always true of other cities. Not only is it difficult to select some restaurants for mention rather than others, fashions come and go. When the present writer first visited Rome, Trastevere was the place to eat: the restaurants there were inexpensive and the food excellent. One could tell the better establishments by the number of seminarians and their professors tucking in: they were in those days, though no longer, distinguish-able by their dark suits and Roman collars. But Trastevere was a victim of its own success and became more expen-sive. Generally speaking, eating places called trattorias are cheaper than ristorantes, though that does not mean they are not as good. Pizzas are widely available, and one can have a snack in an enoteca, as well as buy a bottle of wine (it is really a wine shop).

Meals usually consist of a pasta course ('primo piatto') and a meat course ('secondo piatto'), plus a dessert of some kind. There are some typical dishes. Many will have encountered 'saltimbocca alla romana', veal with ham and sage, but 'abbachio arrosto' – Roman-style roast lamb and a particular favourite of the present writer – is less common outside the city. Another of the author's favourite Roman dishes is 'carciofi alla giudia' or Jewish-style artichokes, small ones, deep-fried, and best eaten in the Ghetto. It is common to be offered a free drink at the end of the meal, a limoncello, an amaretto or, for those who would prefer something less sweet, a grappa. Service is usually added to the bill, but it is polite, if paying with cash, to leave any small change with the waiter. One small oddity, at least to the British: in cafés it costs less to buy a cup of coffee if you choose to stand at the bar, rather than sit down at a table.

## Sleeping

Rome is full of hotels, boarding houses 'pensioni' and other forms of lodging, which vary in price from the very expensive to the rather worryingly cheap. But one relatively safe way to find reasonably priced accommodation is to stay in houses belonging to religious orders. A good number of these rent out rooms to visitors for a modest sum, usually on a bed-and-breakfast basis. They exist throughout Italy (and indeed elsewhere), but there is a surprisingly large number of such convents and monasteries in Rome, often located near pilgrimage sites. They vary in price, and some seem to be little more than hotels – apart from the fact that they often impose a curfew, commonly either 10.30 or 11.00 pm. The easiest way to find these is via the website of Monastery Stays, Italy, which provides a handy map of Rome with these convents marked on it, so that the user can choose the location which most suits. Not all those listed, however, seem to be, strictly speaking, either convents or monasteries, and the user ought to note, in the description given, whether it says specifically that the accommodation is run by one of the Catholic Church's many religious orders. The website (www.monasterystays. com/) also has a form for booking accommodation for groups, as well as for individuals. Another list of convents in which to stay, together with some good advice, can be found on the website of the American church in Rome, Santa Susanna: www.santasusanna.org/comingToRome/convents.html. The North American College also provides a list: visitorsoffice@pnac.org. A popular option is to stay in one of the national colleges, particularly if you are travelling in a parish group or in some other recognizable religious entity. See the section on the colleges (pp. 213–16) for more information, but remember this is more likely to be possible during the summer vacation – when the weather in Rome can be unbearably hot!

## Going to church

Readers of this small book are likely to be doing a great deal of church-going. St Peter's is much visited, and it is quite likely that pilgrims will have to queue, but other churches are easier to get into – up to a point. Apart from the major basilicas, churches have a tendency to shut at midday until perhaps as late as four in the afternoon, and some may not be open at all, perhaps because of restoration work going on inside or because there is no one available to look after them. Dress is important. It is not a good idea for women to have bare shoulders – in some instances they will be handed shawls to cover their upper body. Shorts, on both men and women, used also to be frowned upon, though less so these days. Times of religious services should also generally be avoided, unless of course one wishes to attend.

There are two active Anglican churches in the city, St Paul's within the Walls at Via Napoli 58 (+39 064883339) and All Saints Church at Via del Babuino 153 (+39 0636001881). There is also the Anglican Centre in Rome based at Piazza del Collegio Romano 2 (+39 066780302).

There is a Baptist church at Piazza San Lorenzo in Lucina 35 (+39 066876652), a Methodist church at Piazza Ponte Sant'Angelo (+39 066868314) and a Scottish Presbyterian one at Via XX Settembre 7 (+39 064827627). Obviously there is a plethora of Roman Catholic places of worship, but those with services in English are San Silvestro in Capite (+39 066797775), Santa Susanna (+39 0642014554) and San Francesco Saverio del Caravita (+39 066794560 which is the phone number for the church of Sant'Ignazio). Mass is also available at the English College at 10.00 on Sunday mornings, except during the summer vacation (Venerabile Collegio Inglese +39 066868546). If a large group of pilgrims wish to attend mass at the college, it would be a courtesy to inform the College Rector in advance. More about these Catholic places of worship can be found in the text below.

## Keeping safe

The only time in his life that the present author has been pick-pocketed was while standing on a crowded Roman Metro train. Despite that unfortunate occurrence, Rome on the whole seems no more unsafe than any other large European city, and when walking about in the late evening it feels a good deal more secure than some. It is nonetheless a good idea to leave valuables in a safe at the hotel, but to carry a photocopy of one's passport. It is also advisable to take with you only one credit card and again leave the others, if there are others, behind in some safe place in the hotel.

# 5

# Some Useful Italian Phrases

Guidebooks almost always contain a list of useful words and phrases in the language a visitor is going to encounter. In cities that rely heavily on the tourist trade, such as Rome, many people speak English and often appreciate the opportunity to do so. Listed below, however, are some commonly used phrases to fall back on, or with which to open a conversation. The pronunciation of Italian is not difficult. It is important to remember to pronounce each letter – at least in most cases. Thus 'dove', which means 'where', is not pronounced as if it were the bird but as 'dough vay', and 'dodice', which means twelve (as in Pio XII, Pio dodicesimo), is pronounced 'dough-di-chay'. Otherwise pronunciation is not particularly complicated. Both the letters C and G have two different sounds. Before an E or an I C sounds like the English Ch and G like J (think of 'ciao' and 'gelato'), but otherwise more or less as in English, whereas the Italian Ch sounds like a K and Gh like G (as in 'Chianti' and 'spaghetti'). The combination Gn is pronounced like the English Ni in 'onion', and the letter H is always silent at the beginning of words. There are of course very many other differences between English and Italian pronunciation, but these probably won't cause difficulties for occasional visitors to the country.

| | |
|---|---|
| Good morning | Buongiorno |
| Good evening | Buonasera |
| Good night | Buonanotte |
| Yes/No | Sì/No |
| Excuse me | Scusi or permesso |
| Don't mention it, not at all | Prego |
| Thank you | Grazie |
| Please | Per piacere or favore |
| Do you speak English? | Parla inglese? |
| I don't speak Italian | Non parlo italiano |
| I understand/I don't understand | Capisco/Non capisco |
| How are you?/Fine thank you | Come sta?/Bene grazie |
| On the left/right | A sinistra/destra |
| When will the church open? | Quando apre la chiesa? |
| How much? | Quanto costa |
| Why?/Why not? | Perchè/Perchè no? |
| May I/we have …? | Posso/Possiamo avere …? |
| Breakfast/lunch/dinner | La colazione/il pranzo/la cena |
| I would like | Vorrei |
| Do you have …? | Avete …? |
| Small/medium/large | Piccolo(a)/medio(a)/grande |
| Mineral water sparkling/still | Acqua minerale gassata/non gassata |
| Address/place | Indirizzo/luogo |
| Full board | Pensione completa |
| Bathroom | Il bagno |
| Bedroom | La camera da letto |

| | |
|---|---|
| Toilet/toilets | Toilette or bagno |
| Sir/Madam | Signore/signora |
| Man/woman | Uomo/donna |
| Men/women | Uomini/donne |
| Kitchen/dining room | La cucina/la sala da pranzo |
| A table for two, please | Una tavola per due, per favore |
| A bottle/carafe/glass of red/white/house wine | Una bottiglia/caraffa/un bicchiere di vino rosso/bianco/della casa |
| A glass of beer | Un bicchiere di birra |
| A flavour (of ice cream) | Un gusto |
| A cup of tea/coffee | Una tazza di tè/caffè |
| The bill, please | Il conto, per favore |
| Credit card | La carta di credito |
| Can I use a credit card? | Posso usare la mia carta di credito? |
| Bus/metro stop | La fermata |
| Ticket/tickets | Biglietto/biglietti |
| Return ticket | Un biglietto di andata e ritorno |
| Where can I buy a ticket? | Dove si compra un biglietto? |
| Entrance/exit | Entrata/uscita |
| Push/pull/press | Spingere/tirare/premere |
| Open/closed | Aperto/chiuso |
| How much does it cost to go in? | Quant'è il biglietto d'ingresso? |
| When does it open? | A che ora apre? |
| When does it close? | A che ora chiude? |
| Excuse me, please | Mi scusi, per favore |

## SOME USEFUL ITALIAN PHRASES

| How do I get to ... | Come si arriva a ... |
|---|---|
| Where is/are ... | Dov'è/dove sono ... |
| Is there a map? | Ha una cartina/mappa? |
| Can you show me on the map? | Può indicarmi sulla cartina? |
| Is this the way to ...? | È questa la strada per ...? |
| Cash machine | Bancomat |
| How much is this? | Quant'è questo?/quanto costa? |
| Today/tomorrow | Oggi/domani |
| That's OK | Va bene |

# 6

# Tourist Guides to Rome

This little book is not intended as a tourist guide to the city of Rome. It is only a guide to the main shrines which a pilgrim might wish to visit. The entries will say a little about the sites, usually churches, and their history, but there is of course much more that could be written – and, indeed, has been written about each one of them. And remember, in many, if not most, of the churches listed it will be possible to buy a detailed guidebook to that particular location which will contain not just more information, but rather better pictures than the casual visitor is likely to be able to capture on his or her camera (even when photography is allowed, which is not always). There is a plethora of more general guides, frequently arranged in walks around the city. What follows is just a selection of these, ones that the present author has used from time to time and found helpful.

*Berlitz Guide to Rome*. The smallest in format of any of the guides surveyed below, and rather a seductive purchase for someone unwilling to carry a bulky volume. But it is really far too small for the serious traveller and does not contain a great deal of information, though probably enough for anyone in a hurry.

*Blue Guide to Rome* is in its tenth edition. It is organized by area rather than walks, and is somewhat schematic, though that makes it easy to consult. It contains good maps, in colour, and full colour illustrations. It also has plans of some of the major buildings and under the general rubric of 'Additional Information' suggests places to stay and restaurants in which to eat, with some indication of price. It has an excellent index. Its main drawback is its bulk. It is not something that is easily carried around. There is, incidentally, a *Literary Companion to Rome* in the Blue Guide series, which is well worth a look. It is not a guidebook as such but quotations are drawn from a wide variety of sources about Rome and its sights.

*Companion Guide to Rome* was first published in 1965 by Georgina Masson, and has been revised many times since – it is now in its ninth edition. Its format has changed, and though plump, will now fit into one's pocket. It is arranged by walks, and each walk is accompanied by a map, a rather better map in the latest edition than in earlier ones. It contains illustrations though they are, like the maps, in black and white. It has a wealth of information both historical and cultural, in an easy-to-read style. It now lists the opening hours of the major places to visit, but it does not have general tourist information about buses, where to eat and so on.

*DK Eyewitness Travel Guides: Rome.* It no longer claims on its front cover that the Eyewitness Guides 'show you what others only tell you', but that remains true for it is indeed exceedingly well illustrated. It has excellent maps and a particularly valuable index to Rome's streets. However, it is in a rather large format, too large to be put in one's pocket or handbag. (A basic street index – which is indispensable – can be found in any of the small maps of Rome's transport system widely and cheaply on sale.)

*Everyman CityMap Guides: Rome*. This series is a particular favourite of the present author. It is arranged by areas, gives information about where to stay and where to eat (and shop) and says a little about what sights to visit in each section of the city covered. None of that constitutes its attraction. Its advantage is the comprehensive maps which fold out with ease, and it can easily fit into one's pocket. All that, and coloured illustrations too. It is an excellent additional buy to one of the more heavyweight volumes.

*The Lonely Planet Guide to Rome*. This somewhat beefy volume is, at least according to one bookseller specializing in travel literature, the most popular vade mecum. It undoubtedly has good pictures and plans of galleries and churches. There is also, not something often found, a very creditable history of the city of Rome. There is a pull-out map at the back, which is convenient, and a sensible list of places to visit outside the city. It does not strike one as geared to the pious traveller: when it cites its 13 top sites to visit, only two of them are churches – inevitably St Peter's and the Pantheon, better known to readers of this book as **Santa Maria ad Martyres**, which is only marginally a church. It is described above as 'beefy', and so it is – only just about suitable for the pocket. There is, however, a proper pocket-sized version available.

*Rome: The Early Church: A Pilgrim's Guide*. This little book by Howard Nelson is a publication of the Confraternity of Pilgrims to Rome, and if it is still in print seems to be available only through the Confraternity. At less than 60 pages, it discusses the practicalities of visiting Rome, makes some suggestions as to where to stay (including a campsite), and describes the most ancient churches in chapters divided by century, from Constantine to the early seventh century.

*Rough Guide to Rome.* While this is only just about of a size to fit the pocket there is a pocket-sized version. The text wins plaudits from its users for its clarity and its colour-coded maps and it has much really quite detailed information about the sights, ecclesiastical as well as historical. It is easy to use. Something like a third of it, however, is devoted to eating and drinking and taking trips outside the city so that, to fit in the important material, the typeface is on the small side.

*Time Out Guide to Rome.* In many ways this is similar to the *Lonely Planet Guide*. It does, however, have rather more maps within the text. Like the *Lonely Planet Guide* it has a very useful fold-out map at the back, but in this case the map is in plastic, which could be advantageous in rainy weather. As might be expected from this particular stable, there is really rather a lot on eating and drinking. This is not only regularly updated (most of the guides mentioned here frequently produce new editions), but exists in a variety of forms.

# 7

# Easy Excursions from Rome

The body of this book is concerned exclusively with religious sites. Someone who has come to Rome as a pilgrim might like to take a break from churches and shrines, so a few attractive, easily accessible places to visit from Rome are listed below.

## Castelgandolfo

Rome used to be a dangerous place during the summer months. Several popes died in summer and so did sundry cardinal electors, if a conclave dragged on into July and August. In 1596 Clement VIII acquired a palace in the hills overlooking Lake Albano that had belonged to the Gandolfi family – obviously they gave their name to the town – and had then passed to the Savelli family. Urban VIII had the medieval palace rebuilt by Carlo Moderno, and subsequent popes added to what is, according to the Lateran Pacts of 1929, extraterritorial property of the Holy See. The parish church of St Thomas of Villanova was designed by Bernini. In modern times popes have used it regularly as a summer retreat – though not, at the time of writing, Pope Francis. This could be a matter of concern to the residents of Castelgandolfo because they depend significantly upon the tourist trade. In the grounds of the papal residence is the Vatican Observatory, staffed by Jesuits. Trains run from Stazione Termini to Castelgandolfo. The journey takes approximately an hour. It is also possible to take Metro

Linea A to its terminus at Anagnina and then take a bus. The travel time of the two routes is roughly similar.

## Cerveteri

For those feeling they may have had enough of ancient Romans and would like to try something different, there are always the Etruscans. Two major Etruscan sites are within reach of Rome, Tarquinia and Cerveteri, but the present author has so far visited only the latter. Cerveteri is a small town, and the Etruscan necropolis, a UNESCO World Heritage site, lies just outside it. It was used from the ninth to the third century BC, and covers a substantial area, though only a small part may be visited. There are burial mounds and tombs cut out of solid rock. Some of the tombs have painted interiors and have been fashioned to look like private houses. Indeed, the whole area appears to have been laid out as if it were a small town. To reach Cerveteri, which is some twenty-eight miles north of Rome, one can take a bus either from the Lepanto stop on Metro Linea A, or from Cornelia, the last stop before the train terminus. It has been suggested that Cornelia is the better choice because there is less bus travel through Rome's traffic. The journey from the centre of Rome should take just over an hour, but that depends on the traffic. There is a museum in the town itself, but the best, and for someone staying in Rome the most accessible, display of Etruscan artefacts and statuary is to be found in the Villa Giulia, taking its name from Pope Julius III (1550–55) who had it built originally as a villa for himself. After Julius's death it remained a papal possession, though it was seized by the Italian state after the fall of Rome in 1870, and is now a national museum. It is located at Piazzale di Villa Giulia 9.

## Frascati

Very similar travel arrangements to those above will also take you to Frascati. It is possible to go to Castelgandolfo and return by bus by way of this other hill-top town, popular with Romans who go out there to dine in the fresher air and drink the local white wine. It is very close to the ancient city of Tusculum. From 1761 it was the see of Henry Stuart, Cardinal Duke of York, his first (and effectively only) pastoral charge. He was highly successful and much liked and when as senior cardinal he was perforce made bishop of Ostia, he continued to live in Frascati until his death in 1807. There is a plaque to the man who might have been the last Stuart king of England on the cathedral wall. Because of its location so near to Rome, popes and cardinals built themselves villas to take advantage of the cool climate. The most striking of these is the Villa Aldobrandini which dominates the town centre. The house itself is not open to the public, but visitors can freely walk round the magnificent, though now somewhat dilapidated, garden. To do so, however, it is necessary to acquire a ticket from the tourist office. One of the other villas, the Villa Torlonia, was destroyed during the war by the Allies because it was used by the Waffen SS. It is now a publicly owned park.

## Ostia Antica

According to the very useful website Rome Toolkit (www.rometoolkit.com), the Forum is one of the most popular places to visit in Rome. That is hardly surprising, but for the present author a better sense of what it must have been like to live in ancient Rome is to be had at Ostia Antica, the city at the mouth ('Ostium' means the mouth of a river) of the River Tiber. It is a vast site (in the third century Rome's port is thought to have had a population of 100,000), with houses, streets, shops and tombs. Many buildings still have their mosaic floors worryingly open to the weather. It was here that St Monica, the mother of St Augustine, died in 387 and was buried – though her relics were later transferred to Rome (see **Sant'Agostino**). There is a small charge for entry, and the site is open every day except Christmas Day and 1 May – but never on Mondays. A museum – not wholly inspiring – lies in the middle of the site, and there is a restaurant, so it is possible to spend the whole day wandering around. It is about 20 miles from the city of Rome, and getting there could not be easier. Linea B takes one to Piramide (or Stazione Ostiense – in effect the same place) to catch a train direct to Ostia Antica. The Rome Pass is still valid for this journey.

# PART 2

# *A Note on Using This Book*

The text is concerned chiefly with shrines of one sort or another, and to some extent the physical context in which they are to be found, usually a basilica or a church. Following the text is a list of these shrines, divided into shrines relating to Christ, those relating to the Madonna, and those relating to individual, or very occasionally groups, of saints. Within each division the shrines are listed in alphabetical order. So are the churches, listed by the first word other than Saint, or rather 'Saint' in one of its several Italian forms. The four major basilicas, however, have been put first. At the end of each entry on a basilica or church there is an address. Churches themselves rarely need postal addresses: those that are given commonly refer to the monastery or priests' house from which the church is served. It should, however, be perfectly possible to locate the church itself from the address given.

Stational churches have been marked in the text with an asterisk (*) (see *Glossary*).

# 8

# The Major Basilicas

## *San Pietro in Vaticano (St Peter's)

*The foundation stone of the new St Peter's, replacing the fourth-century basilica, was laid in 1506, but it was not consecrated until 1626. Even then it was not completely finished.*

Surely the world's most famous church, as it stands today St Peter's is the product of the sixteenth and early seventeenth centuries. It is traditionally said to have been founded by Constantine over the grave of the Apostle Peter, a place of pilgrimage for Rome's Christians. Constantine's involvement has, however, been recently questioned – there is very little evidence for it. The original basilica, built on a model similar to the Lateran, probably dates from the years after Constantine, though it was certainly a fourth-century building. By the fifteenth century it was in serious need of repair or reconstruction, and plans were drawn up for this under Nicholas V (1447–55), but it was not until 1506, under Pope Julius II, that work began. As will be noted below in the entry on San Giovanni in Laterano, St Peter's is not Rome's cathedral, but popes have lived at the Vatican, rather than at the Lateran, since their return from exile in Avignon in 1377. There are so many works of art, memorials to popes and so on that the reader of this guide has to remember it is mainly describing this and other churches from the perspective of a pilgrim.

In that context, the first point of interest on entering the piazza in front of the basilica is the obelisk, which was brought from Egypt by Caligula (Emperor 37–41) and re-erected in its present site in 1586 under Pope Sixtus V. It holds, in a reliquary on the top, a relic of the True Cross. On the far right as one faces the façade is the Holy Door, opened only during Holy Years. On entering the basilica the chapel of the Pietà is on the left, Michelangelo's famous statue now being protected by a glass screen. Beyond that is the monument to Queen Christina of Sweden who abdicated in 1654, and who was received into the Catholic Church in Innsbruck on 3 November the following year. She spent much of the rest of her rather turbulent life in Rome, where she died on 19 April 1689. She is buried in the crypt of St Peter's, among the papal tombs.

Next there is a chapel with memorials to Popes Pius XI and Pius XII and the tomb of Blessed Pope Innocent XI (1676–89) – his remains can be seen under the altar – who was beatified by Pius XII in 1956. The supposed remains of St Josaphat, dressed as an Eastern or Byzantine-rite priest, have been placed in the Gregorian Chapel: Josaphat is an entirely mythical character, his life based upon that of the Buddha. In the altar are the relics of St Jerome (347–420), the famously irascible translator of the scriptures into Latin in what is known as the Vulgate. Pope Benedict XIV (1740–58) on the other hand was genial: he is buried in this chapel. Also in the chapel is an eleventh-century painting of Our Lady Help of Christians, or of Bon Secours ('good help').

At the far end of the basilica, in the apse, is Bernini's 'Gloria', which lets light in through an almost transparent alabaster window and illuminates a dove – the Holy Spirit – cradled in a chair. The 'chair of St Peter' is hidden behind this. It is certainly an ancient Roman chair, a pagan one, portraying the Labours of Hercules, but there is nothing to connect it historically to St Peter. Nearby are the tombs of Popes Paul III (1534–49) and Urban VIII (1623–44).

Beyond the high, or papal, altar and to the left is a chapel where Pope St Leo I, Leo the Great (440–61), is buried beneath the main altar. Beside it stands the 'chapel of the column', so called because on a column there is a medieval painting of the Madonna. Here Popes St Leo II (682–83), St Leo III (795–816), and Leo IV (847–55) are buried beneath the altar, with Pope Leo XII (1823–29) lying in the centre. Continuing round on the left-hand side British visitors may well be particularly interested in the memorial to the House of Stuart. Here are interred James III (the old Pretender, 1688–1776), his son the Young Pretender, Bonnie Prince Charlie (1720–88), and Charles's brother Henry, Cardinal Duke of York (1725–1807) who, after Charles's death, would have liked to be known as Henry IX and accorded royal honours, but the pope of the day, wishing to main-tain good relations with Great Britain, would not allow it.

Appropriately close by is the altar where Pope St Gregory I ('the Great', 590–604) is interred in a sarcophagus that can be seen behind a grille: 'appropriately', because it was St Gregory who sent missionaries to England. Also in the chapel is the tomb of the much put-upon Pope Pius VII (1800–23). The chapel contains the relics of St John Chrysostom (c. 347–407), Archbishop of Constantinople and a Doctor of the Church.

Continuing down the same side towards the baptistery there is a chapel with the tomb of Pope St Pius X (1903–14) and the monument to Pope St John XXIII (1958–63), though the tomb of the latter is on the opposite side of the nave and can usually be distinguished by the crowd of pilgrims praying before it. Pope Innocent VIII (1484–92) is buried close by. The tomb of St Peter lies beneath the papal altar and can be approached through the 'confessio' which is in front of the altar. The statue of St Peter, with his extended foot touched or kissed by generations of pilgrims, is to the right when facing the 'confessio': it is believed to have been made in the thirteenth century, possibly by Arnolfo di Cambio.

The great dome over the altar is supported by four pillars, and at the foot of each is a statue. They are of St Helena, Constantine's mother who found the True Cross, and there is a relic of the True Cross; of Longinus, the centurion who pierced Christ's side with a lance and, according to tradition, became a Christian: he is holding the head of the lance; of St Andrew, the brother of Peter, which originally held a relic of his skull, though this has been returned to the Greek Orthodox; and St Veronica who, again according to tradition, wiped Christ's face on the road to Calvary, leaving an image of Christ on the cloth Veronica used: she is holding the cloth. In the crypt can be seen the tombs of Pope Pius XII (1939–58), Pope Innocent IX (1591), Blessed Pope Paul VI (1963–78), Pope John Paul I (1978) and Pope St John Paul II (1978–2005). *Piazza di San Pietro*

# *San Giovanni in Laterano (St John Lateran)

*The façade of San Giovanni in Laterano (St John Lateran), the cathedral of Rome, was erected in the eighteenth century. It is topped by the statues of fourteen saints, seven metres tall, with the figure of Christ in the middle. The high, or papal, altar in San Giovanni in Laterano was constructed in the second half of the fourteenth century. The altar is said to contain the table on which St Peter himself celebrated the Eucharist, and a reliquary at the top is supposed to contain relics of the heads of SS Peter and Paul.*

Ask almost anyone which is the cathedral of Rome and the likely answer is St Peter's. But it is not the Pope's cathedral as Bishop of Rome. Rome's cathedral is St John Lateran, the first Christian basilica to be specifically built as a church, perhaps as early as 313. Constructed on the site of a cavalry barracks – this particular regiment had, unfortunately for them, supported Constantine's rival Emperor

Maxentius – on imperial property, it was intended as the headquarters of the bishop of the city. The name 'Lateran' seems to have been taken from T. Sextus Lateranus, a general of the imperial cavalry, to whom Septimius Severus (Emperor 193–211) gave a house which was still in existence when the basilica was constructed.

In a departure from the strict basilican form it had four aisles but, more significantly, transepts which gave it a cruciform shape. It was severely damaged in an earthquake at the very end of the ninth century and twice destroyed by fire in the fourteenth, as well as being sacked by Vandals and suffering other depredations. It has been consequently much restored, most recently by Borromini during 1646–50, in preparation for the Holy Year of 1650: there is a fresco, attributed to Giotto, which shows Boniface VIII announcing the first Holy Year in 1300. Borromini put a frame around it. It was at the time of Borromini's restoration that the Lateran received its baroque 'makeover'. Until the exile in Avignon, which lasted for much of the fourteenth century, the Lateran basilica and the adjoining palace was the papal residence, but it was in such a poor state of repair when the papacy returned to Rome that the Vatican began to be used in its place.

Because it was the church of the Bishop of Rome many popes were buried there. The tomb of Sylvester II (999–1003), who dropped dead, possibly poisoned, while saying mass in Santa Croce in Gerusalemme, was destroyed in the first of the fourteenth-century fires (1308), but what remained of his relics were reinterred near the entrance to the basilica: there is a cenotaph commemorating him. Borromini also designed tombs both for Sergius IV (1009–12), like Sylvester II possibly assassinated, and Alexander III (1159–81) who died of old age after being driven out of Rome. The tomb of the great Pope Innocent III (1198–1216) is beside the chapel of the Crucifixion: Innocent had died at Perugia and was buried in the cathedral there, but was brought to Rome and a tomb constructed for his remains in 1891. Martin V (1417–31), whose election at the Council of Constance brought the Great Western Schism to an end, is interred in the 'confession' before the high altar. Clement XII (1730–40) is buried beneath the Corsini chapel – he was a member of the Corsini family – in an antique bath that he himself had brought from the Pantheon for this purpose. Leo XIII (1878–1903) was originally buried in St Peter's, but his wish was to be interred in the Lateran basilica and his remains were brought there in 1924: his monument, over the door to the sacristy, recalls his famous encyclical on the 'Conditions of the Working Classes', *Rerum Novarum*. The heads of SS Peter and Paul are supposed to be in a reliquary built into the baldachin over the high altar.

In the altar, it is claimed, is a table, or part of a table, from the house of St Pudens, with whom Peter stayed when he was in Rome. The tradition is that he celebrated the Eucharist on this table. Similarly, it is said that within the altar of the Blessed Sacrament chapel is part of the table at which Christ and the Apostles sat at the Last Supper.

Apart from the relics and the tombs of popes, it has to be remembered that the Lateran basilica is itself an object of pilgrimage. The dedication of the Lateran is celebrated throughout the Church on 9 November and the inscription on its façade reads 'Most Holy Lateran Church, Mother and Head [or Chief, "caput"] of all the Churches in the City and the World'. It is almost always referred to as St John Lateran, but the Roman Martyrology reminds us that the dedication is to Christ the Saviour. This was the original dedication in the fourth century. As visitors will notice, however, next to the cathedral is the baptistery, built at the same time as the basilica, and retaining more of its early Christian appearance than the basilica. This was dedicated to St John the Baptist, and the name transferred to the church from the baptistery. In the twelfth century an additional dedication was made to St John the Evangelist.

Across the road from the basilica is the 'scala sancta', the holy stairs, claimed to be those up which Christ had to walk to reach the place where Pilate was sitting. The steps, 28 of them, are now covered, but glass panels allow the pilgrim to see the red marks, said to be drops of Christ's blood. According to tradition St Helena brought these back to Rome from Jerusalem. The building in which they are housed used to be part of the papal palace, and there is a room at the top of the steps called the Holy of Holies, a private chapel for the pope. Along with many reliquaries there is an icon of Christ which is said to have appeared miraculously. Little is known about it, but it was in Rome by the mid-eighth century when it is recorded that it was carried in procession. The chapels in this building, and there are several, are served by Passionist priests. The basilica itself is served by Canons Regular of the Lateran. *Piazza San Giovanni in Laterano 4*

## *Santa Maria Maggiore (St Mary Major)

The earliest basilica on, or near, this site at the top of the Esquiline was erected under Pope Liberius (352–66) and was consequently known as the Basilica Liberiana. It was, however, entirely rebuilt under Pope Sixtus III (432–40) in honour of the Virgin Mary who had been declared by the Council of Ephesus in 431 to be 'the Mother of God', a title which had been in dispute. It is doubtful whether Sixtus built on exactly the same spot as the Liberian basilica, but the origins of the latter are recalled in the fourteenth-century mosaic to be seen as one approaches the church. It depicts Christ and the Madonna throwing down snow

*The façade of Santa Maria Maggiore, as it now stands, was constructed in the mid-eighteenth century, though some of the original façade survives behind it, including the mosaics. The campanile, several times restored, dates from the fourteenth century (an earlier one had been severely damaged in an earthquake and had to be replaced). It is the tallest in Rome, its appearance enhanced by its location at the top of the Esquiline Hill.*

from heaven, because the story is that snow fell in Rome, miraculously, on 5 August one year, marking out the floor plan of the Liberian basilica, a legend which is commemorated annually by dropping petals from the dome of the Pauline chapel. As a consequence of this story, the church has sometimes been called Our Lady of the Snows. The Holy Door, on the left of the entrance, is only opened during Holy Years.

On entering the church the visitor is immediately struck by the gilding on the roof, said to have been done with the first gold brought to Spain from the New World. Close by the entrance is a monument to Clement IX (1667–69), a popular pope with the people of Rome despite the brevity of his pontificate. He is buried under the floor of the nave. Nicholas IV (1288–92) was also originally interred near the door – he wanted, he said, visitors to walk over him – but during the restoration of the basilica in 1572 his remains were moved to the left of the high altar, and placed in a mausoleum. Pope Sixtus V (1585–90), who did so much to reform the Roman curia, is buried in the Sistine chapel named after him. Interred opposite him is St Pius V (1566–72), the austere Dominican and long-time inquisitor who

*It is unknown how, or when, the relic of the manger in which the infant Christ had been laid in Bethlehem arrived at Santa Maria Maggiore. It was certainly there in the sixth century.*

excommunicated Queen Elizabeth I of England. There is a monument to Pope Paul V (1605–21) in the Pauline chapel which he had created, but he is interred in the crypt, as is his predecessor, Clement VIII (1592–1605), who also has a monument: his sarcophagus was discovered during restoration work in 1942.

The main attraction of the basilica, however, apart from the beauty of the building itself, is the relics of the Nativity, so much so that it was referred to as 'Bethlehem in Rome'. As the name indicates, the basilica is dedicated to the Madonna and her image is present everywhere, especially in the triumphal arch erected by Pope Sixtus III and in the ancient image 'Salus Populi Romani', 'the salvation [or well-being] of the people of Rome', to be seen in the Pauline chapel. The legend is that this portrait of the Virgin was painted by St Luke, and that it was this icon which Pope Gregory I carried in procession through the streets of the city to safeguard it from the plague. It is claimed that the basilica holds relics of the manger in which the Madonna laid Christ after his birth in Bethlehem. It is said that the relics were brought back to Rome after the fall of Jerusalem in 638: they are held in a reliquary above the high altar and are exposed for veneration on the 25th of each month.

Also brought back to Rome were the relics of St Jerome (c. 347–420), the somewhat irascible Doctor of the Church and translator of the Bible, who retired to the Holy Land after a brief stint in Rome. He is buried in the crypt. Also brought back from the Holy Land was the body of St Matthias, the apostle elected to replace Judas Iscariot, who is buried beneath the high altar. In the sacristy is preserved a relic of St Thomas Becket (1118–70), the archbishop of Canterbury who was murdered in his cathedral on the apparent orders of England's King Henry II. *Piazza di Santa Maria Maggiore 42*

# *San Paolo fuori le Mura (St Paul's Outside the Walls)

*This view of the major basilica of San Paolo fuori le Mura was taken from an upper storey of the Beda College, a college for English-speaking and usually older candidates for the priesthood.*

In Roman times cemeteries had to be located outside the walls of the city – hence the grave of St Peter on the Vatican hill, across the Tiber from the ancient city. St Paul was reputedly martyred by being beheaded some two kilometres outside the city: when his head fell, three fountains sprang up as it touched the ground: Tre Fontane, where there is now a monastery. The fountains still flow, though it is clear from archaeological evidence that they were known to the citizens of Rome long before Paul's death. His body was buried closer to the city on the Via Ostia, and a huge basilica was built over his grave towards the end of the fourth century. The basilica was frequently restored, but the present building dates mainly from the nineteenth century: the basilica burned down in 1823 and had to be entirely rebuilt, as far as possible using remaining materials. Not everything was destroyed: the cloisters, a particularly beautiful example, were left intact, as was the baldachin, the work of Arnolfo di Cambio, and a striking medieval paschal candlestick. The mosaics, though

*The interior of St Paul's Outside the Walls. The basilica was destroyed by fire in the nineteenth century and was rebuilt between 1831 and 1854. At the far end can just be seen two survivors: the thirteenth-century high altar and the twelfth-century paschal candlestick to the right of it. Above the columns are the roundels containing portraits of the popes from Peter onwards: there are eight spaces left.*

again much restored, are original. Indeed the whole edifice, despite its reconstruction, is the best example of what an early Christian basilica would have looked like.

As it holds the tomb of the Apostle Paul – a crudely inscribed slab can just about be seen beneath the altar with the words 'Paulo Apostolo Mart' on it – this was one of the major basilicas which pilgrims visited. It also has a set of chains, claimed to be those which fettered the Apostle. In a chapel to the left of the apse is a crucifix which St Bridget of Sweden (1303–73) said spoke to her, and a twelfth-century mosaic of Our Lady before which in 1541 St Ignatius Loyola (1491–1556), the founder of the Jesuits, and his first companions made their formal vows as religious. The basilica is served by a Benedictine community. *Via Ostiense 186*

# 9

# Other Churches and Shrines

## Sant'Agata dei Goti (St Agatha of the Goths)

There is considerable uncertainty about the origins of this church. The name indicates that it was built for the Goths, and an inscription appears to suggest that it was founded by Ricimer (d. 472), a Roman general – his official title was 'magister militum' or 'master of the soldiers' – who effectively ruled the Western Empire for two decades. The Goths were not Catholic Christians but Arians with unacceptable (to the Catholics) views on the nature of Christ's divinity. This would, therefore, not have been a 'Catholic' church, which may account for its abandonment for some years. It looks likely, however, that Ricimer and his fellow Arians took over an already existing church which quite possibly served the Greek community in the city. The early Christian building can still be seen beneath the many restorations. In his *The Christian's Guide to Rome*, Canon Stanley Luff recommended it as a place to rest and meditate.

The dedication to St Agatha, a virgin martyr of unknown date from Catania, or possibly Palermo, was perhaps made ironically: the defeat of the Goths at Catania in 535 being taken as the turning-point in Constantinople's campaign to recover Italy. There are no relics of St Agatha, but beneath the altar are the relics of the martyrs Hippolytus, Adria, Neon and Martia, possibly a married couple and their children. These were brought from Greece and originally interred in the catacomb of St Callistus. There are other, Roman, martyrs in the side chapel dedicated to St Agatha, but it is the group of Greek martyrs who are the main focus of devotion and their feast, on 2 December, is marked by a Catholic Eastern-rite liturgy. The church, which was from 1835 to 1926 the location of the Irish College, then became the Generalate of the Congregation of the Sacred Stigmata ('the Stigmatines') who still look after it. *Via Mazzarino 16 / Via Panisperna*

## Sant'Agata in Trastevere (St Agatha in Trastevere)

For St Agatha herself, see the previous entry. This church is basically an eighteenth-century rebuilding of a much older place of worship, but it has little to commend it in itself. It is, however, the focus for devotion in Trastevere to Our Lady of Mount Carmel. A nineteenth-century statue of Our Lady of Mount Carmel kept in the church is carried through the streets of Trastevere on 16 July, the feast day: she is known as the Madonna de Noantri, 'noantri' meaning 'us and not them' – the 'them' being those Romans on the opposite bank of the Tiber. *Largo San Giovanni de Matha 9*

## Sant'Agnese fuori le Mura (St Agnes Outside the Walls)

This minor basilica is the site of the burial of St Agnes – for whose life story see the next entry – and therefore her major shrine. She was interred in a catacomb, and the church commemorating her was built alongside her burial chamber, so pilgrims have to descend a lengthy staircase to reach the church and to be greeted by the funerary inscription in verse written by Pope Damasus (366–84). It is believed that the first church on this site was built by the Emperor Constantine's daughter Constantina in 342, but as any visitor will immediately observe it is part of a larger complex, the purpose of which is not entirely clear but which may originally have been intended as a mausoleum for Constantine himself. The present church, though much restored over the centuries, was built during the pontificate of Pope Honorius I (625–38) and, despite the restorations, remains very much as a seventh-century Christian would have experienced it. For that alone the church is well worth a visit, though it is some way out of the city. From 1479 the shrine has been in the charge of the Canons Regular of the Lateran, though previously served by a community of nuns.

The relics of St Agnes were placed in a silver casket beneath the high altar in 1615, along with those of St Emerentiana, who is described as her 'milk sister', the daughter, in other words, of Agnes's wet nurse. Emerentiana is reputed to have been martyred while praying at the tomb of Agnes and had her own basilica further along the Via Nomentana on which Sant'Agnese fuori le Mura stands. This was, however, destroyed in the ninth century and her relics enshrined with St Agnes.

In the apse is a fine mosaic from c. 635 which shows the hand of God bestowing the crown of martyrdom on St Agnes. The figure of St Agnes, dressed like a Byzantine empress – though to some extent like a Greek-rite bishop – is flanked by Pope St Symmachus (498–514) who built the first church on the site and is depicted holding a jewelled book and Pope Honorius who is holding a model of the church he built. Though the building is old enough, some things in it are even older: the bishop's chair, for example, and the paschal candlestick which is thought to date from the second century. As has been remarked, the basilica is built into the side of the catacombs, and it is possible to visit these: some of the burial places have not been opened. According to one legend of St Agnes, she appeared eight days after her martyrdom holding a lamb and on her feast day, 21 January, two lambs are blessed, then taken to receive the Pope's blessing before being handed to the nuns of St Cecilia in Trastevere. From these lambs the nuns produce the wool which goes to make the pallia – the symbol of office which the Pope bestows on metropolitan archbishops as a sign of their union with him. *Via Nomentana 364, though the main entrance is at Via S Agnese 315*

## Sant'Agnese in Agone (St Agnes by the Stadium)

The Piazza Navona is one of the great public areas of Rome, its shape determined by the stadium for athletics, the Circus Agonalis (hence 'in agone'), built by the Emperor Domitian and first used in AD 86. The stadium survived well into the fifteenth century relatively intact, its arches frequented by prostitutes as they had been in the early Christian era, a fact which may have influenced accounts of the life of St Agnes, martyred in the stadium in 304. According to the less salacious version she was arrested as a Christian and executed by beheading with a sword because she refused to marry. Another version has her being imprisoned in a brothel and abused, but her hair grew to cover her nakedness, a scene common in her iconography.

At least from the eighth century there was a chapel dedicated to St Agnes based in what was believed to have been the brothel in which she had been held. In the twelfth century the oratory became a church, which was dedicated by Pope Callistus II in 1123. In the seventeenth century the Pamphilij family profited from the election of one of their number to the papacy as Innocent X (1644–55) and not only constructed a palace next door to the church but took over the church itself and completely rebuilt it. The church remained more or less a private chapel until 1992 when it was made over to the diocese of Rome. Splendid though its interior is, the church has no parochial function. A door next to the chapel of St Sebastian leads into the chapel of St Philip Neri, where there is preserved what is believed to be the head of St Agnes. In the chapel of St Francesca Romana there is preserved the font, from the church which the Pamphilij demolished to build this one, in which the saint was baptized. The formal address of the church is on Via di Santa Maria dell'Anima, but entrance is more easily achieved from the Piazza Navona: the church with its striking façade can hardly be missed. *Via di Santa Maria dell'Anima 30 (Piazza Navona)*

## *Sant'Agostino (St Augustine)

The Church of the Augustinian Friars (formerly Hermits of St Augustine) was built from the end of the thirteenth century onwards, next door to an ancient (eighth-century) church of St Tryphon which was eventually demolished in the early eighteenth century to allow the friars' house to expand. It was completed in 1446, but almost immediately rebuilt on a much grander scale, using Travertine stone from the Colosseum to construct the façade. The rebuilding was completed by 1483. Michelangelo began painting his 'Entombment of Christ' for this church, which is a minor basilica, but never completed it: it can now be seen in London's National Gallery. During the early part of the sixteenth century the church served as a meeting place for Rome's humanists, and later as the place of religious observance for Rome's more upper-class prostitutes. On a pillar on the left-hand side of the nave can be found a fresco (much restored) of Isaiah by Raphael, and beneath it a statue of the Madonna and Child with St Anne by Andrea Sansovino before which the humanists were accustomed to read poetry on St Anne's feast day. To the right of the entrance to the church is a statue by Jacopo Sansovino known as the Madonna del Parto, the Madonna of Childbirth, commissioned in 1516 and much venerated by Rome's expectant mothers. An icon of the Virgin Mary, brought from Constantinople at its conquest in 1453, is on the high altar. Traditionally it is said to have been painted by St Luke.

The most highly decorated chapel is, naturally enough, that dedicated to St Augustine of Hippo (354–430) from whom the friars take their Rule. More important, however, to the left of the sanctuary is the chapel and tomb of St Monica (332–87), Augustine's mother, who died at Ostia Tiberina as she and her son were making their way back to Africa. Her relics were brought from Ostia to Rome in 1430 and laid in an ancient Roman sarcophagus. The sarcophagus now stands on the left of the chapel, while the relics themselves were enshrined beneath the chapel's altar. The first chapel to the left of the nave is dedicated to Our Lady of Loreto, and has a famous painting by Caravaggio entitled 'Our Lady of the Pilgrims' ('Madonna dei Pelligrini'), painted 1604–05, in which the artist used a well-known prostitute as the model for the Madonna, thus causing much scandal. *Piazza Sant'Agostino*

## Sant'Alessio all'Aventino (St Alexis on the Aventine)

The dedication of this church is to St Boniface and St Alexis, with Boniface coming first in its official name. This Boniface has nothing to do with the Anglo-Saxon Boniface who was a missionary in what is now Germany, but is a wholly legendary creation.

*This monument in Sant'Agostino was at one time the resting place of the relics of St Monica, the mother of St Augustine, brought here in the mid-fifteenth century. Though the effigy and the late Roman sarcophagus survive in the chapel dedicated to her, her remains have since been interred under the altar.*

According to the legend he was a Roman slave who had an affair with his mistress. They both repented, and Boniface went off to Asia Minor where he was martyred. His former lover had his relics brought to Rome, and she founded a church on the spot. The story of Alexis is equally unlikely: he became a beggar but eventually returned to the family home unrecognized, and lived under the staircase. After his death a paper was found on his body revealing who he was.

The existence of this church before the late tenth century is unclear. In the eighteenth century it was given a major restoration, which is what is to be seen today. A number of different religious orders have had charge of it, but since 1846 it has been in the care of the Somaschi Fathers, an order founded in the sixteenth century by St Jerome Emiliani. In the right-hand aisle there is a large reliquary containing, it is claimed, the wooden staircase under which St Alexis lived: a statue depicts him dying, but holding the piece of paper which revealed his true identity. Above the tabernacle in the Blessed Sacrament chapel, a Byzantine icon from the twelfth or thirteenth century is unusual in that it shows the Madonna in the position of a supplicant, and without the Christ. It is much venerated under the title of Our Lady of Intercession. The crypt contains relics said to be of St Thomas Becket. *Piazza Sant'Alessio 23*

## Sant'Alfonso de'Liguori all'Esquilino
### (St Alphonsus de'Liguori on the Esquiline Hill)

This is a thoroughly nineteenth-century church, designed by an Englishman and paid for by a Scotsman – the latter a Redemptorist priest and eventually Superior General of his Order: St Alphonsus being, of course, the founder of the Redemptorists. The church is of no great interest to pilgrims except for one icon, perhaps the most reproduced icon of Our Lady, and the one to which there is most devotion: the icon of Our Lady of Perpetual Succour (Perpetual Help). This is a specific type of Byzantine icon, one in which the Madonna points to the Child – in this instance the Child is glancing away, looking at the instruments of the Passion which are being carried by two angels. In the fourteenth and fifteenth centuries Crete was particularly known for its school of icon painters, with El Greco, though born in the sixteenth century, being the most famous. This painting is probably fifteenth century, though there is the usual attribution to St Luke. It was somehow acquired by a Roman merchant, brought to his city towards the end of the fifteenth century and eventually placed in the church of San Matteo. That was destroyed during the French occupation of Rome, but the icon was rescued, and when Sant'Alfonso had been built on the site of San Matteo it was handed over

*Sant'Alfonso de'Liguori all'Esquilino was designed by an English architect, paid for by a Scottish Redemptorist priest, Edward Douglas, and built between 1855 and 1858 as the headquarters of the Redemptorist Order. At the time of writing it is the titular church of the archbishop of Westminster, Cardinal Vincent Nichols.*

to the Redemptorists' care. The Order was instructed to foster devotion to Our Lady of Perpetual Succour, something they did with remarkable success. *Via Merulana 26*

## Sant'Ambrogio della Massima
(St Ambrose [of Milan – the 'Massima' is puzzling])

There is a legend attached to this church to the effect that it was built on the house of St Marcellina, the sister of St Ambrose who just about makes it into the Roman Martyrology as 'a virgin of Milan – fourth century'. The earliest records of there being a church or a monastery here are no earlier than the beginning of the ninth century when it was built, or perhaps rebuilt. It was rebuilt again in the twelfth century and yet again in the sixteenth. Originally dedicated to Mary, it seems to have become the church of St Ambrose in the fifteenth century. In a chapel on the left is an icon which it is said was found during restoration work at **San Benedetto in Piscinula**. It is claimed that St Benedict prayed before this icon – in fact a fragment of a fresco. Unfortunately exactly the same claim is made of a similar icon in San Benedetto. Beneath the high altar are the relics of St Polycarp, presumably, though it is not certain, the bishop of Smyrna, who was executed at a great age in, probably, 155. It is known that, after his body was burnt, Christians collected his bones, possibly the first example of Christians' veneration for the relics of martyrs. The church is now in the care of Benedictines of the Subiaco Congregation. *Via S Ambrogio 3*

## *Sant'Anastasia (St Anastasia)

While this minor basilica undoubtedly deserves a mention – after all, St Anastasia, who is alleged to have been martyred in Sirmium (now Sremska Mitrovica in Serbia) during the persecution of Diocletian, is mentioned in the canon of the Roman mass – the church has little in the way of relics (those of Anastasia are now in the cathedral of Zadar in

Croatia) to attract pilgrims, though some appear to have been invented for that purpose. It is, however, open 24 hours, seven days a week for the perpetual adoration of the Blessed Sacrament. It is also the centre of the cult of St Turibius (1538–1606), a law professor in Spain and chief judge of the Inquisition, who was appointed archbishop of Lima, Peru, where he worked with outstanding zeal.

What is most interesting about this church is that it is one of the very earliest, fifth-century, 'tituli' (see Glossary), and the name Anastasia, which means 'resurrection' in Greek, may have come from the original owner of the 'titulus'. It was built into the first floor of an 'insula' or block of dwellings – the word means 'island' – and until comparatively modern times it was necessary to go up steps to enter it. The shops which made up the ground floor of the insula still survive beneath the church. The highly dubious relics were discovered in a lead casket in the fourteenth century, and consist of a coloured mantle, said to have belonged to the Virgin Mary, and a cloak belonging to St Joseph. These, it is claimed, were brought to Rome by St Jerome, as was the chalice which is also preserved. This is an important stational church, where are celebrated the dawn mass of Christmas Day, St Anastasia's feast day and, at one time, the papal Ash Wednesday service, though this is now at Santa Sabina. *Piazza di Sant'Anastasia*

## Sant'Andrea al Quirinale
(St Andrew beside the Quirinale – the Quirinale, formerly a papal palace, is now the residence of the President of Italy)

It is unclear how long a church dedicated to St Andrew has stood on this site, seemingly from at least the twelfth century, but for the most part apparently uncared for. In

1566 the church, in a very dilapidated condition, was given to the recently established Society of Jesus as its novitiate and rebuilt. As the numbers entering the Jesuits continued to grow, the novitiate proved inadequate and it was decided to rebuild yet again. This time the architect was Bernini and the church, finally completed in 1678, is considered one of the finest examples in Rome of the baroque style: Bernini's son claimed that Bernini himself had refused all payment for the work.

The Jesuits were deprived of this church, along with all else, at the Suppression of the Society in 1773 but took it over once more after the Restoration in 1814. The property of the Society was again seized by the Italian government in 1873, shortly after the fall of Rome (1870), along with many other religious buildings. In the case of Sant'Andrea, however, the authorities requisitioned the novitiate as an overspill from the Quirinale, and much was changed, including the room of St Stanislaus Kostka.

Stanislaus (1550–68) was a member of the Polish nobility, but went to Vienna to study under the Jesuits. There he decided to enter the Society but could not do so in Austria so he walked to Rome, where he was admitted. He died, still a novice, after only nine months, having displayed great holiness of life. He was canonized in 1726. His room can still be entered from the church, but it is a reconstruction, though using some of the salvaged original materials. He is buried under the altar of the chapel dedicated to his name. In the chapel dedicated to St Francis Xavier (1506–51) there is the well-known painting by Giovanni Battista Gaulli (1639–1709), known as Il Baciccio, of the great Jesuit missionary dying on the island of Shangchuan on his way, he had hoped, to evangelize China. The Jesuits regained charge of the church in the mid-twentieth century. *Via del Quirinale 29*

*The monument to St Stanislaus Kostka in the church of Sant'Andrea al Quirinale. The church was formerly attached to the Jesuit noviceship, and St Stanislaus (1550–68) died there while still a novice. He was canonized in 1726.*

## Sant'Andrea delle Fratte (St Andrew in the Bushes)

The curious name, which apparently dates from the fifteenth century, suggests that the church was built on what was scrubland – earlier names from the twelfth century would indicate that the church was in a garden. The Minim Friars, who took over the church in 1585 and are still in charge, rebuilt it during the first half of the seventeenth century, but it was completed only in the nineteenth.

It was in the third chapel on the left that Alphonse Ratisbonne (1814–84), a lapsed Jew, had a vision of the Madonna which converted him to Catholicism. His brother had already become a Catholic and a priest, and Alphonse became a Jesuit priest although he left the Jesuits, with the approval of the Superior General, in order to found the Congregation of the Order of Sion, a religious institute to work for the reconciliation of Jews with the Christian faith. Above the altar is an icon of the Madonna as she appeared to Ratisbonne. There is a bust of him on one side of the altar and, on the other, a bust of St Maximilian Kolbe (1894–1941) who was executed in Auschwitz concentration camp after volunteering to take the place of another man who had been condemned to death. *Via Sant'Andrea delle Fratte* 1

## Sant'Andrea della Valle (St Andrew in the Valley)

It is not in fact in a valley. This minor basilica and – now – a titular church was apparently named after a Cardinal Andrea della Valle who died in 1534 and had a palace nearby, but it was also dedicated to St Andrew the Apostle at the request of Costanza Piccolomini d'Aragona, the Countess of Amalfi. She had inherited the Piccolomini palace and the church of St Sebastian and in 1582 handed them over to the Theatine religious order on condition that they were dedicated to Andrew, the patron saint of Amalfi. As a result of the connection to the Piccolomini family the memorials of the two Piccolomini popes, Pius II (1458–64) and the short-lived Pius III (1503), pope for less than a month, were moved to Sant'Andrea from the old St Peter's.

Built between 1590 and 1650, it is a massive church, typical of the Counter-Reformation (the Theatines were created in 1534 to oppose the spread of Protestantism), and has the third highest dome of all Roman churches. To the right of the high altar is a chapel dedicated to the Theatine Cardinal St Giuseppe Maria Tomasi (1649–1713) who is buried there. He was beatified in 1803 but canon-

*The façade of Sant'Andrea della Valle was built
by Carlo Rainaldi (1611–91), a good twenty years
after the church itself had been completed.*

ized only in 1986. He was an enormously learned liturgical
scholar and an ardent reformer of the liturgy, though not
greatly appreciated as such in his own lifetime. The third
chapel on the left is dedicated to St Sebastian. There was a
church on this site dedicated to St Sebastian from at least
the end of the twelfth century. According to legend this
saint, whom arrows failed to kill, was beaten to death in
288 and his body thrown into a sewer on this spot, from
which it was recovered by a Roman matron called Lucina.

As every guidebook insists, the first act of Puccini's *Tosca* takes place in this church. It is still the headquarters of the Theatines. *Piazza Vidoni 6 / Piazza Sant'Andrea della Valle*


## Sant'Angelo in Pescheria
### (The Holy Angel in the Fish Market)

The church was known by this name from at least the end of the twelfth century, by which time there was indeed a fish market beside it, one which survived until the late nineteenth century. It stands in the Porticus of Octavia, a colonnaded area built c. 23 BC by the Emperor Augustus and named in honour of his sister. Within the colonnade were two temples, one of them that of Jupiter Stator, now buried beneath Santa Maria in Campitelli. The colonnade was destroyed several times, and that part of it which now serves as the atrium of the church dates from 203 when it was restored by the Emperor Septimius Severus and his son Caracalla – as it says over the entrance. At some point in the Middle Ages two of the columns holding up the architrave were removed, possibly to be used somewhere else, and replaced by a brick archway.

An inscription at the entrance lists the relics within the church which in 755 – the date in the inscription – was dedicated to St Paul, though the name was changed to the Holy Angel (St Michael) before the end of the eighth century. The inscription, or epigraph, was erected by one Theodotus who described himself as a 'primicerius', the most senior official in a papal administrative department. He had formerly, he says, been a 'dux', which is commonly translated as 'duke' but means a senior military leader, roughly of the rank of general: Theodotus might well have been a general in the papal militia. The church was a diakonia, says Theodotus, a deaconry, whence food was distributed to the poor: it would have been under the charge of a papal official, a deacon, one of those who eventually became cardinal deacons.

In the sixteenth century the church became the church of the confraternity, or guild, of fishmongers, and they built a chapel of St Andrew – a fisherman – at the end of the right-hand aisle. At about the same time Pope Paul IV (1555–59) established a ghetto, one of the gates of which was opposite the entrance to the church. Gregory XIII (1572–85) ordered that on the Sabbath Roman Jews were to hear a sermon preached outside Sant'Angelo.

The interior was remodelled at the very end of the sixteenth century, and there was a further thorough restoration in 1867, so much so that many guidebooks say it is hardly worth visiting. As can be seen, however, it has had an interesting history. It was at the church, for instance, that in 1347 Cola di Rienzo, a parishioner, mustered his troops before attempting to take over Rome and establish a republic. There are various collections of relics within the church. At the time of the 1867 restoration, a marble sarcophagus was placed under the high altar containing the relics of St Cyrus and possibly those of St John of Alexandria who died in Egypt during the persecution of Diocletian (303). The relics of St Symphorosa and her seven sons were brought to the church in the eighth century from the basilica named after her outside the city, which was abandoned possibly because of threatened invasions. They are located near the high altar, together with the relics of the martyrs Zoticus and Amantius, supposedly Symphorosa's husband and son-in-law, but all most likely to be legendary. The church is in the charge of the Clerks Minor Regular, founded by St Francis Caracciola (1563–1608) to engage in works of charity and in perpetual adoration of the Blessed Sacrament. His life is depicted in two paintings on the walls on either side of the high altar. He is not, however, buried at Sant'Angelo, the Clerks having been in the church only since 1909. *Portico d'Ottavia*

## *Santi Apostoli
(sometimes Santi Dodici Apostoli – the Holy Apostles or the Twelve Holy Apostles, the latter being its official name)

This minor basilica was built in the middle of the sixth century, possibly in thanksgiving for the victory of the Byzantine general Narses over the Ostrogoths. The connection with the imperial capital at Constantinople was reinforced by bringing to the church from that city the relics of St James (the Less) and St Philip. Towards the end of the ninth century, when Rome was again under threat, bones of martyrs from outlying cemeteries were brought to city churches, and some certainly came to the Twelve Apostles. The church underwent a major restoration in 1417 by the new pope, Martin V, at the end of the Great Western Schism. Martin was a Colonna, and the Colonna palace is close by – the church was almost a chapel for the family. Another restoration, which amounted to a rebuilding, took place at the beginning of the eighteenth century, and it is that restoration which survives, except that when digging out the old crypt in 1873 the relics of SS James and Philip were rediscovered. They are still in the crypt, under the altar at the far end. Buried in the chapel of St Francis is Lorenzo Ganganelli, the Franciscan Conventual who became Pope Clement XIV and, as pope, suppressed the Society of Jesus (the Jesuits). Also buried in the church is Cardinal Bessarion (c. 1400–72), one of the great scholars of the Renaissance who, as a metropolitan archbishop, had travelled to Italy to discuss reunion between the Churches of Rome and Constantinople. The decision in favour of reunion was much resented in Greece, and Bessarion returned to Italy. The church of the Holy Apostles is in the charge of the Franciscan Conventuals, whose headquarters is next door. *Piazza dei Santi Apostoli 51*

## *Sant'Apollinare (St Apollinaris)

The dedication is to a much revered bishop of Ravenna about whom little or nothing is known. That it exists in Rome is surprising, because for much of the Middle Ages the bishoprics of Rome and Ravenna were rivals. When Italy was ruled from Constantinople Ravenna was the seat of the exarch, or imperial governor. The dedication may perhaps be explained by the wish to gain favour with Ravenna, or perhaps it sprang from the monastery of Greek monks who inhabited this site. The frequently heard suggestion that the name reflects the fact that the church was built on the ruins of a temple to Apollo can be discounted: there is simply no archaeological evidence to support the claim. The church survived, though much restored, until the middle of the eighteenth century, when it was entirely rebuilt.

For some considerable time the complex of buildings at Sant'Apollinare served as the Hungarian-German College, under the governance of the Jesuits, but they now belong to Opus Dei, with the result that the chapels in the church are dedicated to a number of Jesuit saints, and to the founder of Opus Dei, St Josemaria Escrivá, an otherwise unlikely combination. Under the high altar are the relics of a group of martyrs, listed as Tiberius, Eustrasius, Auxentius, Eugenius, Mardarius (or Bardarius) and Orestes, who, with the exception of Tiburtius – and there are several of the same name – do not make it into the standard collections of saints' lives.

The only reason for a pilgrim to visit the church is the fifteenth-century fresco of Our Lady Queen of the Apostles. This had been covered over with plaster, but during an earthquake in 1654 the plaster fell off to reveal the painting. Our Lady was invoked against an epidemic of the plague in 1657, and was credited with bringing it to an end. The fresco has since been removed from its original position at the entrance and placed in a special chapel to the left just inside the church. *Piazza Sant'Apollinare 29*

## *Santa Balbina Vergine (St Balbina)

The dedication is to an unknown saint whose name means 'the stammerer'. Legend has it that she was the daughter of a tribune, Quirinus, who was martyred with her and with a certain Felicissimus, c. 130. Their relics are under the high altar. The church itself, a minor basilica, appears to date from the late fourth century: earlier on in the century it was still a private house. The first sure reference to it being a church, however, comes only in the late sixth century when its priest is named. In the early Middle Ages it became a monastic church, and the building that was the monastery, after many changes of use and much reconstruction, has recently become an old people's home. Within the church is a chapel dedicated to the Franciscan penitent Margaret of Cortona (c. 1247–97) who repented of her time as the mistress of a nobleman and devoted her remaining years to the care of the poor and the sick – and undergoing dramatic mortifications. *Via di Santa Balbina 8*

## San Bartolomeo all'Isola (St Bartholomew)

As the name suggests, this minor basilica is on an island in the Tiber. It is easily reached by a bridge which dates back to 62 BC. The island, which was once crowded with temples, seems to have been used from very early times as a place of healing. There was, for instance, a temple to the Greek god of healing, Aesculapius, whose cult was brought to Rome in 291 BC: it is thought to have been where the basilica now stands. The basilica was built at the very end of the tenth century by the (Holy Roman) Emperor Otto III who dedicated it to his friend St Adalbert of Prague (956–97), who had just been martyred by the 'Prussians' – he died near what is now Gdansk in Poland. Otto had gathered other relics on his way to Rome and they were also enshrined in the basilica. In particular, there are relics of St Paulinus of Nola (c. 353–431), an eminent figure in civic life and who is known, after the death of his child, for his many extant letters to his friends.

The basilica was originally dedicated to SS Adalbert and Paulinus but very shortly afterwards the dedication was changed to that of the Apostle Bartholomew (in the Synoptics, Nathanael in the Fourth Gospel) when the flayed skin of the saint was enshrined there. According to tradition Bartholomew was flayed alive in Armenia, and by a roundabout route his skin came to Benevento where it was seized by Otto II (955–83) and brought to Rome, where he died and the relics remained. His son, the new Emperor, gave them to his church, and they are enshrined in a large and antique bathtub of porphyry which serves as the main altar. In the right wall near the Blessed Sacrament chapel is the bronze casket – actually a Muslim incense burner – in which, it is claimed, the relic came from Benevento. To the left of the altar, in what had once been the sacristy, is the chapel of the Confraternity or Guild of Roman

Millers (the mills themselves floated on the Tiber) and it is in this that the relics of SS Abundius and Abundantius, Exuperantius, Sabinus, Theodora, Marcian and Marcellus are preserved. Abundius was a priest executed at Rome on the Via Flaminia in 304, the others, even more doubtful, supposedly his companions in martyrdom. The relics of St Paulinus are possibly there – possibly, because they were supposed to have been returned to Nola in 1904 though there is some uncertainty about what happened.

Perhaps the most extraordinary thing about this basilica is the presence within the church, before the high altar, of a well. The wellhead is decorated with a carving con- temporary with the building of the church, showing Christ, St Paulinus (or possibly Adalbert), Bartholomew and the Emperor Otto III. The well itself, now dry, goes back to early Roman times and may have been part of the temple of Aesculapius. St Bartholomew is a cathedral because for over two centuries it served as the mother church of the long-disappeared diocese of Porto Santo Rufino. It now serves as a centre of research into modern martyrdom overseen by the community of Sant'Egidio: before that it was served by Franciscans, hence much of the iconography in the building. Before that again it was an Augustinian church. At the beginning of the twelfth century an Englishman called Rahere, who was taken ill while on a pilgrimage to Rome, possibly suffering from malaria, was treated in the hospital attached to St Bartholomew's. So impressed was he with the treatment he received that he, too, became an Augustinian and returned to London to found St Bartholomew's Hospital ('Bart's'). Not sur- prisingly, given its location, the cathedral was frequently flooded and has been much restored both inside and out. The campanile was added in 1118, during the first of these restorations. *Piazza San Bartolomeo, Tiber Island*

## Santi Bartolomeo ed Alessandro dei Bergamaschi
(SS Bartholomew and Alexander of the People
of Bergamo)

This church began life as the chapel of a lunatic asylum,
dedicated, in 1591, to Our Lady of Piety. The asylum was
eventually moved elsewhere, and a confraternity of people
from Bergamo took it over. The former chapel was entirely
rebuilt in the 1730s. The icon of Santa Maria della Pietà,
however, remained, and is installed over the main altar,
and much of the other iconography recalls invocations
from the Litany of Loreto. The first chapel on the right
as one enters the church, which is still administered by
the Bergamese confraternity, is dedicated to Pope St John
XXIII, who of course came from the diocese of Bergamo. A
reliquary below the altar holds one of the Pope's skullcaps.
*Via di Petra 70 / Piazza Colonna*

## San Benedetto in Piscinula
(St Benedict at the Little Pool
[there is no obvious explanation of this title])

The church seems to date from around 1100 and is dedicated to St Benedict of Norcia (c. 480–550), the founder
of Western Monasticism and the author of *The Rule of St
Benedict* which still governs the life of monks in his order.
It has to be said that nothing is known of the saint beyond
what is to be found in the *Dialogues of St Gregory*, and
there is no mention of his having visited Rome, yet, next to
the chapel of Our Lady, visitors are shown what purports
to be his 'cell'. In the chapel there is a fourteenth-century
image of Our Lady with the claim, clearly impossible, that
St Benedict prayed before it (the same claim is made for a
similar icon in **Sant'Ambrogio**). In the apse is a medieval

icon of St Benedict, holding his *Rule*. The church has had a troubled history. It is now cared for by the Heralds of the Gospel, an association mainly of young men and women dedicated to the apostolic life, which was founded early in the twenty-first century in Brazil. There are priests among them. *Piazza in Piscinula 40*

## San Biagio della Pagnotta
(St Blaise 'of the Loaf' – thought to refer to the practice of giving loaves to the poor on the saint's feast day, 3 February)

The church is an ancient one, at least a medieval foundation, but as it survives it dates from the first half of the eighteenth century and is of little architectural interest. However, it preserves a relic of St Blaise. The relic is claimed to be of his throat, rather appropriately as St Blaise, thought to have been bishop of Sebaste in Armenia (Sivas, in Turkey) and martyred in the early fourth century, is the patron saint of those suffering from illnesses of the throat: there is in many churches a blessing of throats on his feast day. Along with the church of San Nicola da Tolentino, this serves as the national church for Armenians. *Via Giulia 64*

## San Bonaventura al Palatino
(St Bonaventure on the Palatine)

The dedication of this church is to St Bonaventure (c. 1218–74), the Franciscan Doctor of the Church. The foundation of the friary, however, was the work of another Bonaventure, a widower, born Miguel Gran in Barcelona in 1620, died in Rome in 1684 and beatified in 1906. He began a reform movement among the Franciscans, one of several which eventually amalgamated to form the modern Friars Minor. One member of this movement was St Leonard of Port Maurice (1676–1751) – the 'Port Maurice' comes from the name of his birthplace, Porto Maurizio in Liguria. He was the Guardian of St Bonaventure's, and a great preacher. He also erected sets of the Stations of the Cross, one in the Colosseum which is no longer there, and one in the street leading to the friary which can still be seen – though St Leonard's originals deteriorated quite quickly and were replaced in 1772. St Leonard is interred beneath the high altar, while the crucifix he used during his preaching tours can still be seen to the right of the altar. His room in the friary can be visited. The remains of the Blessed Bonaventure are in the Lady Chapel. *Via San Bonaventura 7*

## San Callisto (St Callistus)

The life of Pope St Callistus (d. 222) was more than usu-ally dramatic for a prominent churchman of the early third century. He was a slave, entrusted with running a bank which it seems he defrauded and then went on the run. When he was captured he was imprisoned but on release was given charge by Pope Zephyrinus of the catacomb – the cemetery – which still bears his name. He was then elected pope and finally martyred, it is claimed, by being thrown down a well in Trastevere. The small church, founded in the eighth century but rebuilt in the early years of the seven-teenth century, is itself not of great interest and is sometimes omitted from guidebooks. However, it is claimed that it was constructed on the site of Pope St Callistus's house, and that the well in which he was drowned is beside the church. It still has water. *Piazza San Callisto*

# San Carlo ai Catinari
(St Charles [Borromeo] 'in the district of the
dish makers')

This is largely a seventeenth-century building which serves
as the headquarters of the Barnabites, or the Clerks Regular
of St Paul, an order founded in the church of St Barnabas
in Milan in the sixteenth century by St Antonio Maria
Zaccaria. Charles Borromeo, now a Doctor of the Church,
was in charge of the archdiocese of Milan and was patron
of the Order, hence the church is decorated with numerous
depictions of the life of Borromeo. To the right of the apse
is the chapel of Our Lady of Providence, which houses a
painting of the Madonna as Our Lady of Providence, produced about 1580, to which there is great devotion: the
painting on display is a copy, the original stored elsewhere
for safe-keeping. The picture, by Scipione Pulzoni, inspired
Elena Bettini to found in Rome in 1832 the Daughters of
Divine Providence. *Piazza Benedetto Cairoli 117*

# San Carlo al Corso
(St Charles [Borromeo] on the Corso)

It should be noted that the formal name of this rather
large, early-seventeenth-century church is 'St Ambrose
and St Charles on the Corso', both the saints having been
archbishops of Milan, and the church being the replacement for a church of the Confraternity of Lombards in
Rome. The Confraternity technically owns the church,
but it is administered by Rosminians. In 1614 the heart
of Charles Borromeo (1538–84), who had been canonized in 1610 as one of the great reforming saints of the
Counter-Reformation (or Catholic Reformation, the term
is somewhat controversial), was donated to the church

*St Charles Borromeo (1538–84) was canonized in 1610, which was the occasion for the building of the church of San Carlo al Corso, though it was not completed until 1684. In 1614, however, St Charles's cousin, Cardinal Federico Borromeo, gave the saint's heart to the church, where it is enshrined in the ambulatory behind the high altar.*

and can be found in a chapel in the ambulatory behind the main altar. There is a chapel dedicated to St Olav or Olaf (995–1038), the King of Norway who helped to bring Christianity to that country. Consequently this church is the national church for Norwegians in Rome. *Via del Corso 437*

## San Carlo alle Quattro Fontane
(St Charles [Borromeo] at the Four Fountains)

Sometimes known as San Carlino, or the 'Little St Charles', it is indeed a small, though very beautiful church of which the architect was Francesco Borromini. It was originally founded on a small chapel dedicated to St Charles very shortly after his canonization, but was entirely rebuilt by the Spanish branch of the Trinitarians, an order founded near Paris at the end of the twelfth century by St John of Matha to ransom slaves from captivity to the Moors. The monastery of the Trinitarians was finished quite quickly, but the construction of the church dragged on from the 1630s to the 1680s, during which time Borromini had committed suicide: the story has it that his wish to be interred in the church was rejected by the clergy because he had taken his own life. Though, like **Sant'Andrea al Quirinale**, it was sequestered by the Italian government after the fall of Rome, the popularity of the church preserved it for the Trinitarians.

Of particular interest to pilgrims is the shrine of Elizabeth Canori Mora (1774–1825) whose relics are enshrined under the altar of the Barbarini chapel. A married woman, she was born and died in Rome and suffered abuse from her violent husband. In 1801 she unexpectedly recovered from a very serious illness, an event which turned her towards works of charity, and she began to have mystical experiences. She joined the Trinitarian order of nuns despite the fact that her husband was still alive: she foretold that he would repent his violence towards her – which he did after her death and also became a Trinitarian, though he died as a Franciscan. She was beatified in 1994. *Via del Quirinale 23*

## Santa Caterina della Rota (St Catherine of the Wheel)

This church has existed since at least the first half of the twelfth century, but only from the end of the fifteenth did its name become St Catherine after the (legendary) saint of Alexandria who was martyred by being broken on a wheel. The present building dates from the end of the sixteenth century, and is of little interest apart from a statue of Our

Lady with St Anne, her mother according to tradition, which used to be carried in procession around the streets and is an especial object of devotion for pregnant women. It is worth mentioning that the church is the responsibility of the Archconfraternity of the Palafrenieri – the grooms or stablemen of the papal court. Their original church was Santa Anna, now just inside the Vatican City, but they were given Santa Caterina when the Vatican City was established. *Via di San Girolamo della Carità 80*

## *Santa Cecilia in Trastevere (St Cecilia in Trastevere)

St Cecilia (the Latin form sometimes used is Caecilia) is one of the many third-century Roman martyrs about whom everything we know is drawn from a much later account which is almost certainly wholly fictional. According to this legend she had committed herself to a life of chastity but was required to marry. She told her husband-to-be, Valerian, of her wish to remain a virgin. He respected this and himself became a Christian, along with his brother Tibertius, and both were martyred. Cecilia buried them, and then was herself arrested and condemned to death by suffocation in her own bathroom by the steam being turned up to scalding. She survived, and the soldier then sent to behead her attempted three strokes of his sword without severing her head. She died three days later and was buried in the catacomb of St Callistus by a Bishop Urban (possibly Pope St Urban I, 222–30), who then turned her house into a church. Her body was discovered incorrupt in the catacomb by Pope Paschal I (817–24) who said she was wrapped in a cloth threaded with gold and laid in a coffin of cypress wood. Paschal built the present church and placed the saint's coffin, which he lined with silk, in a marble sarcophagus. In 1599 the sarcophagus was opened:

the body, in a silk-lined coffin and still wrapped in a cloth with gold thread, was found within. Carlo Maderno (1556–1629) was present and claimed that his sculpture, which is now in the sanctuary of the church showing Cecilia lying on her side with her head turned away, represents what he saw at the time. This rather long explanation is necessary to understand the church and the shrine.

The present church, a minor basilica, is a much restored version of that erected by Pope Paschal who is depicted in the apse mosaic. It stands on a fifth-century church of which only the baptistery has been found. On the right-hand side of the present church is a chapel known as St Cecilia's bath house, presumably inspired by the legend. What is now the crypt was, in all probability, the 'confessio' when the church was erected in the ninth century. It was, however, reconstructed at the very beginning of the twentieth century and the relics of Cecilia, Valerian, Tibertius and Maximus – a soldier who was sent to arrest Valerian and Tiburtius but who himself converted to Christianity – were enshrined there. Along with these, supposed relics of Popes Urban I and Lucius I (253–54) were also placed in the crypt.

In 1530 the neighbouring monastery was given to a community of Benedictine nuns who spin the wool from the lambs which are blessed at **Sant'Agnese fuori le Mura**, and then weave the pallia to be distributed to newly appointed metropolitans as a sign of their unity with the Pope. A conservatoire, the Accademia di Santa Cecilia, was located here from 1562 to 1651: Cecilia is, of course, the patron saint of music, and is frequently depicted with an organ in the background. It is unclear why she has this particular patronage, though it may be that it comes from the antiphon for her feast day which says 'as the organs were playing [at her marriage to Valerian] she sang in her heart'.

*Piazza di Santa Cecilia 22*

# Chiesa Nuova ('The New Church')

*St Philip Neri (1515–95) was the founder of the Congregation of the Oratory, and this shrine with the saint's effigy is to be found in the Chiesa Nuova which was built for the Oratorians and opened in 1577.*

Or so it is commonly called, but the dedication is to Our Lady and St Gregory the Great, and the official name is Santa Maria in Vallicelli which is thought to mean the church of Our Lady in a Little Valley. However, the translation is disputed, because it is not obvious that it is in a little valley. The original church on this site is believed to date from the end of the sixth century, that is from the time of Pope Gregory I (590–604), but there was certainly one from 1179 which had fallen into disrepair when it was handed over to the founder of the Oratorians, St Philip Neri (1515–95), in 1575. Work on the building continued until 1590 – though the façade and campanile were added later – and the vocations of aspirants to the new Order were tested by St Philip when he required them to take part in the building work, manual work of the sort young members of the nobility usually thought beneath them. The house of the Oratorians is to the left of the church.

In the middle of the façade is a Madonna and Child, and on either side statues of St Gregory and St Philip. St Philip is entombed, in a crystal casket, below the altar of his chapel, which is to the left of the high altar. Over the high altar is a thirteenth-century icon, regarded as miraculous, of Our Lady of Vallicelli. It is, however, hidden behind a painting of the Madonna with angels by Peter Paul Rubens, who also painted the two canvases on either side, depicting the martyrs whose relics are enshrined here, including SS Domitilla, Nereus and Achilleus. The church is decorated, at the request of St Philip, with images of the life of the Virgin. With the permission of the sacristan it is possible to visit St Philip's room by taking a staircase in the left transept. *Via del Governo Vecchio 134 / Piazza della Chiesa Nuova*

## *San Clemente (St Clement's)

This minor basilica has been served, since the seventeenth century, by Irish Dominican friars. Strictly speaking this is St Clement's by the Lateran because there is another St Clement's in Rome, but 'San Clemente' invariably refers to this ancient church which stands upon even more ancient foundations. First, however, it is important to understand who this St Clement was. There is a letter, the First Epistle of Clement, sent from the Christian community in Rome to that in Corinth towards the end of the first century – making the letter one of the oldest Christian documents, probably older than some parts of the New Testament. It is sent by someone called Clement, a fairly common name, on behalf of the community – he seems, in other words, to be its secretary. Nonetheless the earliest succession lists place him after Linus and Anacletus as a successor to Peter as Bishop of Rome, an anachronistic title. A later legend has him being exiled to the Crimea, drowned by having an anchor tied to him (his symbol, therefore, is an anchor),

*The sixth-century schola cantorum, the place for the singers, in the centre of San Clemente comes from the early medieval church which lies beneath the present twelfth-century one. In the apse Christ is depicted as the Lamb of God, while the apostles on either side are shown as sheep.*

but the waves miraculously gave up his body and his relics were brought back to Rome in the ninth century by Cyril and Methodius, the apostles of the Slavs. These supposed relics were then interred in this church – or rather, its predecessor. There was certainly a church dedicated to St Clement in Rome by the end of the fourth century, though not necessarily on the same site.

Beneath the church there is a Mithraeum – a shrine to the god Mithras – with an associated 'school' for those wishing to be initiated, and a much larger building, likely to have been a storehouse of some kind. The fourth- or early-fifth-century church made use of part of this building. The earlier church, or part of it, still survives beneath

*It is easy to miss the entrance to San Clemente, which is just off a main thoroughfare and, because the road was raised, is behind an atrium below the level of the surrounding buildings.*

the present one and can be visited (as can the Mithraeum): the present one, consecrated in 1108 during the pontificate of Pope Paschal II, has been constructed on top of it. There are suggestions that the earlier church had been damaged by vandals, or by fire or an earthquake. If it had been damaged at all prior to the rebuilding, apart from the natural depredations of age, it was probably by an earthquake, but it may have been necessary to raise the level of the floor of the nave because it was liable to flooding. In the middle of the twelfth-century church is the 'schola cantorum', the place for the singers, which comes from the earlier church and was salvaged during the reconstruction. It can be dated to the pontificate of Pope John II (533–35) who had served in the church as a priest. His name was Mercurius, but this being the name of a pagan God he changed it on his election, the first pope known to have done so.

In the 'confessio' beneath the high altar are the supposed relics of St Clement and also those of St Ignatius of Antioch, martyred c. 107 in Rome. He was the first to write about the role of bishop – he appears to have taken charge of the church in Antioch c. 69 – and to speak of the 'Catholic' church, meaning the church wherever it existed. Something is known of his life and theology through the seven letters he wrote while being escorted to Rome to meet his death, though nothing is known of his actual martyrdom. St Servulus is interred in the chapel of the rosary – a devotion, of course, of which Dominicans are especial protagonists. Nothing is known of him beyond the story told by Pope St Gregory I (590–604), that he was a beggar who used to plead for money at the church door, but then would share his earnings with others. There is a chapel dedicated to the brothers Cyril and Methodius, the apostles of the Slavs. Cyril (826–69) died in Rome and was almost certainly buried in the early church, but he was not regarded as a saint until 1880, and his relics were not transferred to the medieval basilica: there is a fresco depicting his funeral. There are many depictions of the lives of these saints – and of the early popes – both in the early and, more particularly, in the later church. *Via di San Giovanni in Laterano / Piazza San Clemente*

## *Santi Cosma e Damiano (SS Cosmas and Damian)

Dedicated to two Arab doctors who were, according to tradition, martyred in Cyrrhus in 302 during the persecution of Diocletian, the church was erected by Pope Felix in 527, using a hall, possibly a library, which had been part of the Temple of Peace in the Forum. The church was originally a diaconia, a centre for the Church's charitable activities in the city. Before that, however, it had served as the headquarters of Rome's medical services, which may account for the dedication to the two doctors, who are named in the (Roman) canon of the mass. The sixth-century apse mosaic, depicting the Second Coming of Christ, is one of the finest in Rome. The saints, who supposedly were twins, are buried in the crypt. The church can only be visited from within the Forum. Friars of the Regular Third Order of St Francis have looked after the church since the early sixteenth century. *Via dei Fori Imperiali 1*

## Santa Costanza (St Constance)

The first thing to be said is that there was never a St Constance. The fourth-century building within the same complex as **Sant'Agnese fuori le Mura** was originally a mausoleum for Constantina, the daughter of the Emperor Constantine (or possibly in the first instance for the

Emperor himself, before he went off to Constantinople). The sarcophagus of the supposed saint is now in the Vatican, with a replica in the church itself. The arcade is decorated by some very beautiful fourth-century mosaics which have little or no Christian content, though in the niches around the walls there appear to have been Christian mosaics from a slightly later period. Only two now survive.
*Via Nomentana 349*

## San Crisogono (St Chrysogonus)

There are many puzzles about this minor basilica in Trastevere, not least the dedication. Though he is mentioned in the Roman canon, Chrysogonus was a martyr in Aquileia in the far north-east of Italy c. 304, and was especially venerated in what is now Serbia. Details of his life are drawn from the wholly legendary life of St Anastasia (also mentioned in the Roman canon) who was martyred at around the same time in Sirmium, the modern-day Sremska Mitrovica in Serbia, though her relics were later transferred to Constantinople. The relics of Chrysogonus may have been venerated in this church since the fifth century, though the church itself is older. There is a possibility that this 'titulus' was founded by someone called Chrysogonus and the relics brought there because of the similarity of name. There are, it should be said, supposed relics of the same saint in Venice, but the Roman ones can be seen in a reliquary beneath the high altar.

In the middle of the highly decorative ceiling is a painting of the Apotheosis of St Chrysogonus by the seventeenth-century artist Giovanni Francesco Barbieri (Guercino): at least, this version is said to be a copy. The original, looted by the French during their occupation of Rome, was sold on and is now in the ceiling of the Long Gallery at Lancaster

House in London. In the left aisle of the basilica is the body of Blessed Anna Maria Taigi (1769–1837). She was born in Siena but came to Rome seeking work. She married a butler and bore seven children, but was abused by her husband. She gained a considerable reputation during her lifetime for holiness, and her spiritual advice was much sought after. She was beatified in 1920. Her corpse is dressed as a Trinitarian tertiary – the church is in the care of the Trinitarians – and some of her belongings are preserved as relics in the Trinitarian house next to the church. It is possible to visit what remains of the first church on this spot by going down a staircase in the sacristy. There are frescoes which date from the sixth century recounting the legend of SS Chrysogonus and Anastasia. Archaeologists are undecided whether this building was constructed as a church, or had some other function and was converted into a Christian meeting-place. *Piazza Sonnino 44*

## Santa Croce e San Bonaventura dei Lucchesi
(The Holy Cross and St Bonaventure of the People of Lucca)

The first church on this site was erected at an uncertain date and dedicated to St Nicholas of Myra ('Santa Claus'). The second church was built on top of the original one, which became the crypt. A third church was built in the sixteenth century after it had been handed over to the Capuchins, who appear to have used the second church as their choir: they dedicated their new church to the Franciscan St Bonaventure. The iconography of the church refers either to the saints of Lucca, whose 'national' church this became, or to the Capuchins. One notable Capuchin who was a member of the community, and who died here, was St Felix of Cantalice but his shrine was moved to **Santa Maria**

**della Concezione dei Cappuccini** when the Capuchins took up residence there. The church is now looked after by the Sisters of Mary Reparatrix and their founder, the Belgium-born Mary of Jesus (Émilie d'Oultremont van der Linden d'Hooghvorst, 1818–78), is enshrined in the chapel dedicated to the Trinity. Blessed Mary of Jesus – she was beatified in 1997 – only became a nun after the death of her husband. She had four children, and died not in one of her convents but in the house of one of her sons. *Via dei Lucchesi 3*

## Santa Croce in Gerusalemme
(The Holy Cross in Jerusalem)

*The rather impressive façade of Santa Croce in Gerusalemme was added in the eighteenth century. Behind it can be seen the medieval campanile with a curious clock: it lacks a minute hand.*

This basilica originally formed part of the Sessorian Palace (the word simply means 'residence'), home possibly to the Emperor Constantine before his departure for Constantinople and certainly to his mother St Helena. It was St Helena who, according to tradition, travelled to the

Holy Land and there identified the cross on which Christ had been crucified: the name, Santa Croce, which became common only in the Middle Ages, indicates that a relic of the cross was venerated there. The chapel of St Helena is said to have been the saint's private chapel within the Sessorian Palace though there is some suggestion it may have been her bedroom, and where the relics Helena brought back were first venerated. The earliest name for this church, created out of the great reception hall of the palace, was 'Jerusalem at the Sessorian Palace' and there was a story that great quantities of soil had been shipped from the Holy Land to form the floor of Helena's chapel. It was regarded as so sacred a place that until the twentieth century women were not allowed to enter!

Given the great age of the basilica – the palace pre-dates Constantine by almost a century – it has gone through many restorations, and a complete baroque makeover in the middle of the eighteenth century. It has also had many different religious orders looking after it, the Cistercians being the last. The Cistercian community, however, was judged by Pope Benedict XVI to have become so dissolute that it was dissolved in 2011, the abbot having been deposed two years earlier.

Close to the entrance to the church on the right-hand side is a verse epitaph to Pope Benedict VII (974–83) who first established a monastic community here. According to the epitaph, the Pope is interred in the wall of the nave. Many of the frescoes which decorate the building refer to the life of St Helena, though she is herself buried in a separate funerary basilica outside Rome on the Via Labicana. Nonetheless the relics of Christ's Passion which she is credited with bringing to Rome are still in Santa Croce. The statue of Helena in her chapel is a statue of the Roman goddess Juno with head and hands replaced, and a cross added.

Next to the chapel of Helena is that of Pope St Gregory the Great (Gregory I) with an astonishing reliquary holding the alleged relics of some two hundred saints, and in the middle of the reliquary, which is in the form of a triptych, there is a mosaic of the suffering Christ. It is of uncertain date, but thought to be thirteenth or fourteenth century. It is said to represent the figure of Christ as he appeared in a vision to Pope Gregory, who then went on to paint what he recalled. There is no mention of any such vision in Gregory's copious writings. According to tradition, a mass said at the altar in this chapel will immediately liberate a soul from purgatory – hence depictions of purgatory in the decoration of the chapel.

The relics once in the chapel of St Helena were moved to a separate chapel at the end of the left aisle. Most of them have to do with the Passion of Christ: thorns from the crown of thorns, a nail from the cross (the nail is at least of the correct period), fragments of the True Cross, part of the cross of the Good Thief, part of the pillar of the scourging of Christ and the 'titulus', the inscription which Pilate ordered to be placed on the cross. It appears that this relic was hidden in the wall of the church in the middle of the fifth century and forgotten about, being rediscovered only in 1492 during some restoration work. Also among the relics is the finger, it is claimed, of St Thomas the Apostle, 'Doubting Thomas', the finger which he demanded to put into the side of Christ, a scene depicted in the chapel of St Thomas in the church. Below the high altar there is an urn containing the relics of SS Caesarius and Anastasius. *Piazza di Santa Croce in Gerusalemme 12*

**Domine Quo Vadis**, a pilgrimage church, *see* **San Sebastiano fuori le Mura** *Via Appia Antica 72*

## Santi Domenico e Sisto (SS Dominic and Sixtus II)

Little is said about this church in most guidebooks, beyond drawing attention to the particularly splendid staircase that leads to the entrance. It is effectively the chapel of the Dominican-run university in Rome, the Angelicum (the famous Dominican theologian St Thomas Aquinas (c. 1225–74) was and is known as the 'Angelical Doctor'), and is not therefore always open, certainly not during the summer vacation. This church was a long time in construction, from 1575 to 1663, on the site of an early medieval church and it was intended to house Dominican nuns from the church of **San Sisto Vecchio**. The new building was therefore to be called San Sisto Nuovo, but it was realized that there was no church in Rome dedicated to the founder of the Order of Preachers (therefore OP), better known as Dominicans, St Dominic Guzman (c. 1170–1221). Hence the dual dedication. Pilgrims, particularly those associated with the Dominican family, will be interested in the relics of Blessed Hyacinthe-Marie Cormier (1832–1916) which are enshrined above the high altar. A noted preacher and retreat-giver, he was Master General of the Dominicans from 1904 until shortly before his death, and was largely responsible for what became the Angelicum. *Largo Angelicum 1*

## Santa Dorotea (St Dorothy)

The original dedication of this church was to St Sylvester. St Dorothy was added in the fifteenth century, and then it was dedicated solely to her. She was from Caesarea in Cappadocia, where she was martyred in 304. According to the legend, on her way to execution she was mocked by a certain Theophilus who demanded she send him fruits from paradise when she got there – an angel duly delivered and Theophilus was converted and also put to death for his faith. This was a very popular story in the Middle Ages and is illustrated in this, as it now stands, eighteenth-century building. The supposed relics of St Dorothy, present here since 1500, are enshrined under the main altar. For those interested in the Catholic revival of the sixteenth century, the Oratory of Divine Love, founded by St Cajetan (1480–1547) in 1517 in the sacristy, was one of the turning-points of reform. Cajetan went on to found the Theatines with Giovanni Pietro Carafa who later became Pope Paul IV. *Via di Santa Dorotea 23*

## Sant'Eusebio all'Esquilino
(St Eusebius on the Esquiline Hill)

Given that in the early Church there were many people, including a number of saints, who were called Eusebius, it is surprising that the one who gave his name to this church is regarded as never having existed. There are 13 listed in the Roman Martyrology, a number which includes the dedicatee, though it simply says that he is the 'titular'. This was a very early church, certainly in existence by the fifth century. It was several times restored, rebuilt in the thirteenth century, and again in the eighteenth. It has been claimed that the building of the church was paid for by St Eusebius of Bologna, who as the Martyrology remarks was a friend of St Ambrose in his battle against Arian heretics – in other words, Eusebius of Bologna flourished in the latter half of the fourth century. If he did finance the building, that makes the church very old indeed even if nothing really ancient can now be observed. This St Eusebius's relics are enshrined in the high altar, or so it is believed. The church fronts the Piazza Vittorio Emanuele, not far from Termini station. On 17 January, the feast day of St Anthony the Abbot, animals, now entirely pets of one sort or another, are blessed in the piazza. Note that there used to be a monastery attached to Sant'Eusebio. This is now a police barracks. *Piazza Vittorio Emanuele 12A*

## Santa Francesca Romana (St Frances of Rome)

*The church of Santa Francesca Romana is built on the ruins of a pagan temple. Although it appears to be within the Forum, it cannot be entered from there but only from the road outside.*

The official name of this church, located just off the Via Sacra in the Forum, is Santa Maria Nova, but it is generally known as Santa Francesca Romana. Santa Maria Nova ('the new Our Lady's') was constructed in the mid-eighth century because the original Santa Maria Antiqua was thought to be falling down. It was built on the site of two back-to-back temples to the goddesses Roma Aeterna and Venus Felix which had been erected by the Emperor Hadrian (AD 76–138, Emperor from 117). The original dedication was to SS Peter and Paul and commemorated a battle between St Peter and the would-be magician Simon

Magus (cf. Acts of the Apostles chapter 8, but the story was embellished in later apocryphal writings such as the Acts of Peter) when Simon was defeated by Peter's prayers: stones bearing the imprint of Peter's knees as he knelt in prayer are preserved in the church.

Frances of Rome, Francesca Bussa de' Leoni (1384–1440), was a devout married woman who cared for the poor and homeless of the city. She became an oblate of the Olivetan Benedictines who looked after the church, and founded an enclosed order of women oblates which still survives. She entered her foundation after the death of her husband. As an oblate, after her death her body was claimed by the Olivetans and was enshrined in the 'confessio' in front of the main altar, where it can still be venerated.

Pope Gregory XI (1370–78) is entombed in the church, placed there at the expense of a grateful citizenry because it was he who brought the papacy back from Avignon. In the apse above the altar is a twelfth-century icon of the Madonna and Child. When it was cleaned in 1950 it was discovered that it had been painted over a much earlier icon of the Madonna and Child, possibly from the sixth century and therefore one of the earliest known icons of Our Lady. This ancient icon – the origin of the title 'antiqua' – is now preserved in the sacristy. Also in the sacristy, and of particular interest to British visitors, is a portrait of Pope Paul III (1534–49) who is shown talking to the English Reginald Pole (1500–58), whom Paul III created a cardinal in 1537, and who served as archbishop of Canterbury under Queen Mary (1516–58, Queen of England from 1553). The picture does not show him in cardinatial robes, so it was presumably painted before his elevation. *Piazza di Santa Francesca Romana 4*

## San Francesco d'Assisi a Ripa Grande
(St Francis by the River – the usual title in English,
though the Italian means 'at the great shore [or bank]')

The Franciscans have proved down the centuries to be a
somewhat fissiparous religious order, and now exist in
three main forms, namely Friars Minor, Conventuals and
Capuchins. This church, however, precedes the various
divisions. It began life perhaps early in the twelfth century as
a hospice for pilgrims to Rome, looked after by Benedictines.
In 1229 it was handed over to the Franciscans but by that
time St Francis of Assisi (1181–1226) had already stayed
in the hospice, which seems to have been inhabited informally by his followers even before it was formally theirs:
the cell in which the saint stayed can still be visited. The
Franciscans rebuilt the church in 1231 and rebuilt it again in
the first decade of the seventeenth century. When this latter
rebuilding apparently threatened the continued existence of
Francis's cell, the saint appeared in a vision to the cardinal
who was funding the work, and the cell was preserved.

As might be expected, the iconography within the church
reflects the lives of Franciscan saints, although under the
altar of the chapel of the Holy Family there is a wax figure
purporting to be the martyr St Leontia of whom abso-
lutely nothing is known: even the name is 'provisional'
as the reliquary admits. The relics of St Charles of Sezze
(Giovanni Carlo Marchioni, 1630–70) are enshrined in
the chapel of St Michael. He was a Franciscan lay brother,
canonized in 1959, towards whom there is a particular
devotion in Rome because of the work he did among the
poor of the city. Interred in the chapel of St Anne is the
Blessed Ludovica Albertone (1473–1533), a pious widow
and Franciscan Tertiary, who also spent her life aiding the
poor of Rome. She is commemorated by a Bernini sculpture. *Piazza San Francesco d'Assisi 88*

## San Francesco di Paola ai Monti
(St Francis of Paola on the Hills)

This is a seventeenth-century church which serves as the headquarters of the Minims (see **Santissima Trinità dei Monti**) who were given the palace next door as their convent: it had been the residence of the Borgias. The church is not of great interest and is in any case likely to be shut. It contains the shrine of Blessed Nicola Saggio (1650–1709), a Minim friar originally from Lombardy who became so popular in the ministry in Rome that he was sent to Calabria where he is reputed to have worked many miracles. He returned to Rome just before his death. His canonization was urged on the Pope by, among others, James III, pretender to the throne of England. This church has been named the national church for Italians from Calabria. *Piazza di San Francesco a Paola 10*


## San Francesco Saverio del Caravita
(St Francis Xavier of Caravita)

The unusual name 'Caravita' is derived from the name of the Jesuit Pietro Garavita who built a small church here in 1631 (there had been an earlier church which had fallen into ruins) from which he and a team of Jesuits were intending to evangelize the peasants who came into Rome from the countryside to find work. It was much enlarged, indeed rebuilt, in 1677. It holds a relic of Francis Xavier (1506–51), one of the first disciples of the Jesuits' founder, St Ignatius Loyola. Francis Xavier became a famous missionary in the Far East and is enshrined in Goa. The church also deserves a mention because the community associated with it, not all of them Jesuits, is English-speaking, and they provide a high-quality English liturgy and have strong ecumenical links. *Via del Caravita 7*

# The Gesù

*The church of the Gesù (as it is always known) is the chief church of the Society of Jesus, and used to be the society's headquarters, though the Jesuit Order is now administered from Borgo Santo Spirito, much nearer the Vatican.*

This is the most important of all the churches of the Society of Jesus (the Jesuits) and is dedicated to 'the most holy name of Jesus', but is always known as 'il Gesù'. It served as a model for Jesuit churches around the world, but it can also be described as the first church of the Catholic Reformation, with its wide nave and unrestricted view of the high altar: it was built for preaching and for the laity to be able clearly to witness the liturgy. After several false starts, construction began in 1568. Though its interior is very far from austere, the baroque decoration was added in the second half of the seventeenth century and was not part of the original design.

*This icon enshrined within the church of the
Gesù is known as the Madonna della Strada,
Our Lady of the Street. The founder of the
Jesuits, St Ignatius Loyola (1491–1556), had
a particular devotion to it.*

The founder of the Society of Jesus, St Ignatius Loyola
(1491–1556), is buried in a magnificent tomb in the left
transept, topped by a globe in lapis lazuli. His relics are in
a gilded bronze urn beneath the altar. The statue above the
altar was originally entirely of silver but it was damaged as
a consequence of the French occupation of Rome, either
directly by soldiers or possibly melted down on the orders
of Pope Pius VI to pay off Napoleon. Ignatius (originally
Iñigo) had been a courtier in the service of the royal house

*The chapel of St Ignatius Loyola within the church of the Gesù. It was built between 1695 and 1699 under the direction of Andrea Pozzo (1642–1709), a Jesuit lay brother. Pozzo was responsible for several other churches and, most spectacularly, for the 'dome' of the church of Sant'Ignazio – which is not a dome at all, just an optical illusion (trompe-l'oeil).*

of Castile and later of the Duke of Najera. He underwent a conversion after being wounded by a cannon ball at a siege of Pamplona and, after a period spent as a hermit in a cave in Manresa, near Barcelona, he went to study at the University of Paris. There he gathered a small group of followers who formally became a religious order in 1540.

The best known of these followers is the missionary St Francis Xavier (1506–52), whose monument (he is buried in Goa though there is a reliquary containing one of Francis's arms) is directly opposite. Xavier was born in the Castle Xavier in Navarre, and met Ignatius at the University of Paris. He arrived in Goa in 1541 as a missionary and travelled to what is now Sri Lanka and to Japan. He died on an island off the coast of China while trying to reach the Chinese mainland: the painting above the altar depicts the saint's death.

Next to the chapel of St Ignatius there is a smaller chapel which contains a fifteenth-century painting known as the Madonna della Strada, 'Our Lady of the Street'. It was originally in the church of Santa Maria degli Astalli which was demolished to build the Gesù and was the church the first Jesuits took over when they arrived in Rome and began to preach to the 'people of the street'. Next door to the church is a residence which was the Society of Jesus' headquarters until this moved to Borgo Santo Spirito, behind the colonnades to the left of St Peter's as one stands looking at it. It is possible to visit the Gesù residence to inspect the small rooms in which Ignatius spent his life directing his new order, and writing to its members around the world. The altar at which the saint said mass the day he died can still be seen there. *Via degli Astalli 16 / Piazza del Gesù*


## San Giorgio e dei Martiri Inglesi
(St George and the English Martyrs)

This is Rome's national church for the English. It is located near the Spanish Steps and is attached to a small convent of the Poor Servants of the Mother of God, founded in England in the nineteenth century. Apart from its association with England, this twentieth-century church is of no intrinsic interest to pilgrims. *Via San Sebastianello 16*

# *San Giorgio in Velabro (St George in Velabro)

English pilgrims seeking relics of their national patron saint to venerate need to visit this church where can be found his skull, spear and flag. The relics are ancient; they were brought to this church from the Lateran under Pope Zacharias I (741–52), though it is much more questionable whether they go back to George's death, thought to have been in Lydda, in Palestine, c. 303. It is often said that he only became widely known as a result of the Crusades, but his cult, especially among Greeks (and this church for a long time in the Middle Ages served a Greek community), was widespread, including in Anglo-Saxon England. It is true, however, that it became a major part of the English tradition only after Richard I (the Lionheart) put his crusaders under the saint's protection, and in 1222 his feast day, 23 April, was made a holiday.

The church itself is ancient, and retains much of the ancient layout, though the building has been much remodelled. It appears to have been built first during the pontificate of Leo II (682–83) when it was dedicated to St Sebastian as well as to St George, St Sebastian being thought to have saved the city from plague a couple of years earlier. There is an apse mosaic thought by some to be the work of Giotto (c. 1266–1337). The relics of St George can be seen in the 'confessio' under the altar. When Blessed John Henry Newman was created a cardinal deacon in May 1879, San Giorgio in Velabro was his titular church. The name remains puzzling. The 'velabrum' from which the church gets its title was a busy commercial area of Rome, but it is not at all clear what the meaning of the term is – it is thought to be pre-Latin. The church is now served by the Canons Regular of the Holy Cross, 'the Croziers', a religious order more than eight centuries old which, at its origins, also had links to the Crusades. *Via del Velabro 19*

# *San Giovanni a Porta Latina
## (St John at the Latin Gate)

*This little chapel of 'St John in Oil' (San Giovanni in Oleo) was built in 1509. It commemorates the legend that St John the Evangelist was ordered to be boiled in oil on this spot, but when that did not kill him, he was exiled to the island of Patmos.*

This rather out-of-the-way church, administered since 1939 by the Rosminians who have their Generalate next door, would in itself not qualify for entry into this book because there is no shrine there. However, attached to it is a small oratory of St John. The origins of the church are unknown, as is its date of construction, but it would seem to have been built around the year 500. It has, naturally enough, been restored many times. It owes its dedication to the belief that St John the Evangelist was brought to Rome as a prisoner, was on this spot boiled in oil but emerged from the cauldron unscathed, and was then exiled to the island of Patmos where he wrote the Apocalypse (the Book of Revelation). Needless to say there is no evidence for all this, though it is true the story arose very early. It is also not certain that all the New Testament authors called John are one and the same. However, that aside, the precise site where the boiling in oil is supposed to have taken place is now marked by the small chapel, or oratory, called San Giovanni in Oleo, St John in Oil, which may very well have been erected at the same time as the church, but was entirely rebuilt in 1509. *Via di San Giovanni a Porta Latina 17*

## San Giovanni Calibita (St John Calibytes)

The saint to whom this church is dedicated is said to have been a nobleman of Constantinople who became a monk and travelled to Italy, where he lived – with other Greek monks – in caves or shacks which were known as 'kalybe' in Greek. This was in the ninth century, though an alternative version places the saint in the fifth century. His body was found when the church was rebuilt in the middle of the seventeenth century and is now enshrined under the altar. This church is attached to **San Bartolomeo all'Isola**. *Isola Tiberina 39*

## *Santi Giovanni e Paolo (SS John and Paul)

The early history of this minor basilica is complicated. It stands alongside a roadway known as the Clivus Scauri, or Scaurus' Rise ('scaurus', it should be explained, means 'swollen ankles'). Beneath the church are two Roman houses which can be – and ought to be – visited. They were clearly in Christian ownership and used for worship. The

*The basilica of SS John and Paul (Santi Giovanni e Paolo), though much restored, dates from the fifth century. The portico seen here, however, is from the middle of the twelfth century.*

original owner was a senator called Byzans, but it was his son Pammachius who gave his name to the 'titulus'. There is no reason to doubt the existence of Pammachius: he was known to St Jerome as a patrician who was generous to the poor and quite possibly built the church in the late fourth or early fifth century. Originally listed as the 'titulus' Pammachius, a century or so after it was opened its name was changed to the present one. The change was made to dedicate it to two saints who, according to the accounts of their martyrdom, were retired soldiers called back into service under Julian the Apostate, Emperor during 361–63, and put to death for refusing to offer sacrifice to the gods. They were buried secretly, but then, according to an even later version of their deaths, Crispus, Crispinianus and

Benedicta came to pray at their tomb, and were themselves caught and martyred: this scene of martyrdom is to be found in a fresco in the house under the basilica. The supposition is that Byzans or his son began to build a church over the place of their burial, and there are indeed tombs within these houses, something extremely unusual because it was forbidden to bury people, apart from Vestal Virgins and the imperial family, within the city walls.

The relics of John and Paul were placed under the high altar in the middle of the eighteenth century, during one of the several restorations of what is still basically a fifth-century basilica. Also in the mid-eighteenth century the basilica was handed over to the Congregation of the Passion (the Passionists) and it has been under their care ever since. St Paul of the Cross (1694–1775), the founder of the Order in 1720, had rooms in the monastery attached to the basilica, and his shrine is in the very obvious domed chapel in the basilica. The Blessed Dominic Barberi, who joined the Passionists in 1814, lived for some time in this monastery before introducing the Passionist Order to Britain, and receiving Blessed John Henry Newman into the Church. A further British connection is the portico – it was commissioned for the church by Pope Adrian (or Hadrian) IV (1154–59): Nicholas Breakspear, so far the only English pope. *Piazza dei Santi Giovanni e Paolo 13*

## San Giovanni Battista dei Fiorentini
(St John the Baptist of the Florentines)

The church was built in the sixteenth century as the 'national' church in Rome of the people of Florence. It is a distinguished Renaissance church with a baroque façade. St Philip Neri (1515–95), himself from Florence, was the parish priest of this church from 1564 to 1575, and here

founded the Congregation of the Oratory. He is commemorated in a chapel on the right. In the museum, though
formerly located over the sacristy door, is a statue of John
the Baptist, originally believed on stylistic grounds to be the
work of Donatello, but now known to be by Michelangelo.
It is here that the blessing of lambs takes place at Easter.
*Via Acciaioli 2*

## San Giovanni della Pigna
(St John [the Baptist] of the Pinecone)

The pinecone in question has not for a long time stood
outside the church but was moved into the Vatican gardens
where it is still to be seen. The dedication to John the
Baptist stems only from the seventeenth century when the
church was rebuilt. The earlier church had been dedicated
to SS Eleutherius and Genesius whose relics were enshrined
though they were later moved to **Santa Susanna**. Some
relics of St Genesius survive in the church, however, and
are under the main altar. Genesius seems to have been
martyred in Arles in 303. According to his legend he was a
public official who fled Arles when the proclamation of the
persecution of Christians – he was a catechumen – was read
out, but was later captured and beheaded. The Romans,
however, claimed him as their own, saying that he was
an actor ('Genesius the Comedian') who was acting in an
anti-Christian play when he was suddenly converted. The
original church on this site dates from at least the middle of
the tenth century, and some elements of the medieval building survive in the later structure. *Vicolo della Minerva /
Piazza della Pigna 51*

## San Girolamo della Carità (St Jerome of Charity)

The name of this church needs some explanation. Its dedication is to St Jerome (c. 347–420), a Doctor of the Church and the person responsible for the translation of the Scriptures into the standard Latin text, the Vulgate. There is a tradition that while Jerome was in Rome from 382 as secretary to Pope St Damasus I he lodged in the house of St Paula (347–404) which was believed to have been on the site now occupied by the church.

The church was originally built for Franciscan Observants, but after they moved out it was taken over by the Confraternity of Charity, a society of aristocrats with a particular concern for prisoners in a nearby gaol. Because these were laypeople the Franciscan convent was empty, and it was taken over by a group of secular priests, one of whom was the Florentine St Philip Neri (1515–95), who joined the community of priests at the church on his ordination in 1551. It was here that he founded the Congregation of the Oratory (Oratorians). Even after his followers had moved out to the Chiesa Nuova St Philip remained at San Girolamo for some years, where he used rooms located over the transept for living quarters, to receive visitors and give spiritual direction. After his canonization they were turned into a chapel, and are known to the Oratorian Fathers as 'the First Oratory'. In theory the rooms are open to visitors, but since the priests of Opus Dei took over the church – their university, the 'Athenaeum of the Holy Cross', is next door – access has been problematic and the church is rarely open. This is a pity, because the decoration is very beautiful. St Oliver Plunkett (1625–81), the martyred archbishop of Armagh, lived in the community here in 1654. San Girolamo is located directly opposite the Venerable English College. *Via de Monserrato 62A*

## San Giuseppe dei Falegnami
(St Joseph of the Carpenters)

This church stands in the Forum, above the Mamertine Prison where, it is claimed, St Peter was held before his execution, something which is perfectly possible. The prison cells are entered via the porch of the church and can be visited even when the church itself is closed – it usually is. Immediately below the church is the Chapel of the Crucifix and below that again is the death cell, originally entered through a hole in the roof but now accessible via a staircase. Detention in prison for a crime was not a Roman practice: the cells themselves were used as places of execution or for holding prisoners before they were taken to be thrown off the Tarpeian Hill or to other sites of execution. The cell associated with St Peter has been turned into a chapel: San Pietro in Carcere, St Peter in Prison. *Clivo Argentario 1*

## San Gregorio Magno al Celio
(St Gregory's on the Coelian Hill)

English pilgrims should have a particular interest in this church for it was originally the home of Pope St Gregory the Great (590–604). He converted it into a monastery dedicated to St Andrew (the church is still officially St Andrew and St Gregory) and lived there as abbot before becoming pope. It was to this monastery that he brought Anglo-Saxon boys, purchased as slaves in the market, to be trained as missionaries to England, though in the end in 596 he sent Augustine, the prior of the monastery, instead with 40 monks. Gregory was a great admirer of St Benedict, and was the first monk to be pope, though it would be an anachronism to call his monastery Benedictine. Benedictine monks took over in the tenth century, however, and after a somewhat chequered history the church and adjoining monastery are now administered by Benedictine monks of the Camaldolese Congregation.

The church itself was renovated many times in the Middle Ages, then again in the mid-seventeenth century and also the eighteenth. At the end of the right aisle is the chapel of St Gregory. A room off the chapel is claimed to be Gregory's original cell, with a chair on which he sat, while behind a grille is the stone on which, reputedly, he slept. Otherwise little or nothing of the original foundation survives in the church except possibly a fresco of the Madonna, said to be the one that spoke to him. In the garden, however, are three chapels, two of which are medieval. One, dedicated to St Barbara, claims to be the dining room where Gregory fed the poor, and inside is a marble table which dates from before Gregory's time. Beside it is a chapel dedicated to St Andrew. The chapel of St Sylvia, Gregory's mother, dates from the early seventeenth century. Although the guide-books do not mention it, the church is, unfortunately, rarely to be found open. *Piazza di San Gregorio 1*


## Sant'Ignazio (St Ignatius)

This church, built between 1626 and 1685, was constructed to commemorate the canonization in 1622 of Ignatius Loyola (1491–1556), the founder of the Society of Jesus (the Jesuits). It was designed by a Jesuit priest, Orazio Grassi, its ceiling decorated by a Jesuit lay brother, Andrea Pozzo, who was a master of *trompe l'oeil*. There is a mark in the nave where one should stand to get the best view of the ceiling, which represents the entry of Ignatius into heaven, together with other notable achievements of the Jesuits. St Robert Bellarmine (1541–1621), who was

*The high altar of the Jesuit church of St Ignatius
(Sant'Ignazio). The paintings in the apse are by Andrea
Pozzo (1642–1709), a Jesuit lay brother, and depict
scenes from the life of Ignatius. The church was meant to
serve the students of the Jesuits' Roman College, now the
Gregorian University.*

an eminent theologian and a cardinal and, from 1931, a Doctor of the Church, is buried in the third chapel on the right. In the right transept there is a particularly splendid tomb of St Aloysius (Luigi) Gonzaga (1568–91) who entered the Society contrary to his family's wishes and who had Robert Bellarmine as his spiritual director. St Aloysius is the patron saint of young people and it is sometimes possible to visit his room by way of a staircase near his altar. St John Berchmans (1591–1621), another young Jesuit saint, is buried in a tomb on the left transept. *Via del Caravita 8A / Piazza di Sant'Ignazio*

## *San Lorenzo fuori le Mura
(St Lawrence Outside the Walls)

The early history of this basilica is difficult to determine, but it probably began in the fourth century with a shrine abutting the catacomb where the martyr St Lawrence was buried. Lawrence was a Roman deacon closely associated with Pope Sixtus II (257–58) who was put to death a few days before him. The role of a deacon was to attend to the welfare of the poor in the Christian community, so in addition to the symbol of the gridiron, on which (the highly unlikely) tradition has it he was roasted to death, he is sometimes depicted as holding a purse from which to distribute alms. The church over the shrine was built during the pontificate of Pelagius II (579–90) but a church dedicated to Our Lady had already been constructed nearby in the pontificate of Sixtus III (432–40). Given the fame of St Lawrence, his shrine was an extremely popular pilgrim destination for which Pope Clement III (1187–91) provided a hospital as well as adding the campanile and a cloister. Finally Honorius III (1216–27) linked up the church dedicated to Our Lady with that built by Pope

*The present basilica of St Lawrence Outside the
Walls (San Lorenzo fuori le Mura) was built during
the pontificate of Pope Honorius III (1216–27). It
underwent many restorations, but after it was bombed
during World War II (it is close to Rome's marshalling
yards) the portico was put back very largely to how it
would have looked when first constructed.*

Pelagius, the former providing the nave, the latter the chan-
cel, together with the martyr's shrine: it is easily possible
to see the join. There were various other developments of
less moment, but the front of the basilica was damaged by
an Allied bombing raid during World War II (the basilica,
as pilgrims will discover, is not far from Stazione Termini,
and Termini's marshalling yards were the target). For the
most part the damage has been well restored.

The shrine of the saint is under the high altar. With the
relics of St Lawrence are those of – supposedly – St Stephen,
the protomartyr, which had been brought from Jerusalem
to Constantinople and then, by Pope Pelagius, to Rome.
The triumphal arch depicts Pelagius holding a model of the

*The shrine, below the main altar of St Lawrence Outside the Walls, is that of two martyred deacons, St Stephen, the protomartyr, whose relics were brought to Rome in the time of Pope Pelagius II (579–90) and St Lawrence himself, martyred in Rome in 258.*

church, together with Lawrence, Stephen, Peter and Paul – and St Hippolytus (martyred 235) who is the only antipope to be treated as a saint (whether he was an antipope, and whether the martyr wrote the works attributed to him, are much debated questions). At the far end of the basilica is the tomb of Blessed Pope Pius IX (1846–78) under whom the Papal States, including Rome itself, were finally lost to the forces of King Victor Emmanuel whose 'wedding cake' monument stands in the Piazza Venezia. By the time of his death Pius IX had become extremely unpopular with the people of Rome, who threatened to throw his body into the Tiber. At the entrance to the basilica is a seventh-century sarcophagus in which, tradition has it, the body of Pope Damasus II was interred in 1048. The first church was built upon a field belonging to the Emperor Lucius Verus (130–69, Emperor from 161), hence the area was called the Campo Verano: from 1837 down to recent times it has been the main cemetery in Rome. The church is under the charge of the Franciscan Friars Capuchin. *Piazzale del Verano 3*

## San Lorenzo in Damaso

The name means 'the church of St Lawrence in the house of Damasus', Damasus being the Pope from 366 to 384 who, despite now being regarded as a saint (as most of the early bishops of Rome are), was elected after a particularly violent confrontation between his supporters and those of another candidate. He was, however, a cultivated man and reorganized the papal archives and library: both are very likely to have been kept in this church. He was interested in the cult of martyrs and restored the catacombs as pilgrimage sites, providing previous popes and some of the martyrs with epitaphs inscribed on marble. He is buried under the high altar. The church, which is a titular church and a minor basilica, is not easy to find as it is entirely surrounded by the Cancelleria, a palace originally built for Cardinal Raffaele Riario but confiscated by Pope Leo X (1513–21) when Leo discovered that the Riario family had been plotting against him. It then became the Roman Church's chancellery – hence the name. The church of San Lorenzo was rebuilt at the time the Riario palace was being constructed: the entrance is by way of a nondescript doorway at the north end of the piazza on which the Cancelleria stands. It has been so often restored that there is little of interest apart from Damasus's tomb. Students of papal history might, however, be interested to know that Pellegrino Rossi, Pius IX's Prime Minister who was assassinated in 1848, is buried here. *Piazza della Cancelleria 1*

## *San Lorenzo in Lucina

Despite its antiquity, this is not one of Rome's more interesting minor basilicas, having been many times rebuilt or restored. It is first mentioned in the year 366 as the place where Pope Damasus (366–84) was elected. The 'titulus' 'in Lucina' suggests that it was originally based on or in the property of a woman called Lucina, and the church is indeed built upon an 'insula' or tenement block. The dedication is to St Lawrence, the deacon who was supposedly executed in the third century by being roasted on a gridiron. He has a chapel, the first one on the right-hand side of the nave, and the alleged gridiron, or part of it, is to be seen through a bronze grille in the altar. The most striking feature of the church is the crucifixion scene by Guido Reni, painted c. 1640, which serves as the altarpiece of the main altar. It was not originally intended for the church but was donated in 1669, and inspired much devotion. The French painter Nicolas Poussin (1594–1665) is buried in the second chapel on the right. *San Lorenzo in Lucina 16A*

## *San Lorenzo in Panisperna
(St Lawrence in Panisperna – the name of the street is thought to refer to the practice of distributing bread, 'panis', and jam, 'perna', to the poor)

The site of this church is thought to have been the location of St Lawrence's martyrdom, and that would suggest there has long been a place of worship at this spot, but little evidence survives. Whatever was here before almost entirely disappeared in the sixteenth-century rebuilding. Pilgrims will be interested to see the 'oven' in which St Lawrence is alleged to have suffered, located in a chapel just at the entrance to the church.

# Colour section captions

1   The foundation stone of the new St Peter's, replacing the fourth-century basilica, was laid in 1506, but it was not consecrated until 1626. Even then it was not completely finished.

2   It is unknown how, or when, the relic of the manger in which the infant Christ had been laid in Bethlehem arrived at Santa Maria Maggiore. It was certainly there in the sixth century.

3&4   The icon 'Salus Populi Romani'. 'Salus' means health or salvation, but in this context the phrase could be translated as 'Protector of the Roman People'. Picture 3 shows the icon's location within the Cappella Paolina (it was begun by Pope Paul V, hence the name) within Santa Maria Maggiore, picture 4 the icon itself. Because it has been restored several times, it is difficult to judge the age of the painting, but according to tradition in 593 it was carried in procession by Pope St Gregory I to plead for an end to the plague.

5   The Scala Sancta. Traditionally said to have been brought to Rome by St Helena, the mother of the Emperor Constantine, they are claimed to be the steps ascended by Christ as he entered the Praetorium to appear before Pilate. Made of marble, they are now covered in wood and may only be climbed on one's knees.

6   The interior of the basilica of St Agnes on the via Nomentana, built by Pope Honorius I (625–38) over the catacombs in which the saint had been buried, though her relics were later enshrined under the high altar. She is depicted in the apse, with Honorius on one side and Pope Symmachus (498–514) on the other.

7   The Madonna del Parto, a statue in the basilica of Sant'Agostino by Jacopo Sansovino (1486–1570). The title comes from the inscription over the head of the Madonna: 'Virgo tua gloria partus', which means 'Virgin, your glory is in giving birth'. It has been a focus in Rome for the devotion of expectant mothers.

8    The curious monument to St Alexis in the church
     dedicated to him on the Aventine. According to the
     legend of the saint he had left home as a teenager and
     when he eventually returned was not recognized by his
     parents. For the remainder of his life he slept under a
     staircase, represented in the monument, at his parents'
     house.

9    Our Lady of Perpetual Succour (Help), perhaps the most
     famous icon in the Catholic world, is to be found in
     the church of Sant'Alfonso de'Liguori. It is a fifteenth-
     century painting by a Cretan artist and has been in
     Rome since the end of that century.

10   The monument to St Cecilia by Carlo Maderno
     (1556–1629), who claimed to have depicted the saint
     as she was found when her sarcophagus was opened in
     1600. It is to be found in the church dedicated to her.

11&  The shrines of two Jesuit saints in the church of
12   Sant'Ignazio. Picture 11 shows St Robert Bellarmine
     (1542–1621), a cardinal and a Doctor of the Church,
     picture 12 St Aloysius Gonzaga (1556–91), who died
     caring for victims of the plague while studying for the
     priesthood.

13   The high altar of the basilica of Santa Maria dei
     Miracoli with the miraculous icon enshrined above it.

14   The famous statue of St Teresa of Avila in ecstasy by
     Gian Lorenzo Bernini (1598–1680), which shows a
     cherub about to pierce the saint's heart with a lance. It is
     to be found in the church of Santa Maria della Vittoria.

15   The high altar and apse of the church of Santa Prassede.
     The apse mosaic depicts Christ flanked by SS Peter and
     Paul and the sister-saints, Pudentiana and Prassede, who
     are dressed as princesses. On the left with the square
     halo, indicating that he is still alive, is Pope St Paschal I
     (817–24). He is holding a model of the church which he
     had built.

16   This third-century fresco from the catacomb of St
     Priscilla seems to show a woman with her baby – the
     earliest known depiction of the Madonna and Child.

I

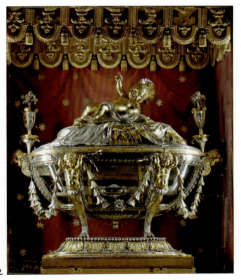

2

4

5

6

7

8

9

10

11

12

13

14

15

16

Inside are buried the brother martyrs SS Crispin and Crispinian, died c. 285, whom tradition, though no evidence, claims were apostles of France and – possibly – of Britain. Their feast day is 25 October, the day on which occurred the battle of Agincourt, hence the speech Shakespeare puts into the mouth of King Henry V (Act 4 Scene 3). St Bridget of Sweden (1303–73) was buried in a chapel on the left which is still dedicated to her: she used to come to pray at the church, and distribute alms to the poor outside it, but her body was later transferred to the abbey she had founded at Vadstena in Sweden. Now interred in the chapel is the Roman virgin and martyr Victoria who reputedly died in the persecution of Decius, but of whom nothing is known. The church is in the care of the Franciscans. *Via Panisperna 90*

## Santi Luca e Martina (SS Luke and Martina)

St Luke the evangelist is traditionally believed to have been an artist (there is a painting in the church which shows him at his easel). He was therefore the saint to whom the church was dedicated when it was granted to the 'Academy of St Luke', founded in 1577 as an association of artists. The church was first built in the sixth or seventh century, at which time it was dedicated to St Martina, martyred in 226 or thereabouts. She was believed to have been the daughter of a Christian consul, and even to have been a deaconess at an earlier church on this site. When she was beheaded, the story goes, her body bled milk, as a consequence of which she is venerated as the patron of nursing mothers. Her relics were in the first church; when, in the middle of the seventeenth century, the church was being rebuilt and a tomb excavated in the crypt for the then head of the academy, her relics were found and reinterred beneath the altar in

*We speak of the 'Roman Forum', but strictly
speaking there were several of them, and the
church of SS Luke and Martina, originally built
in the sixth or seventh century, stands on one of
them. It was rebuilt between 1635 and 1671.*

the crypt. Also in the crypt is a chair on which popes sat
when distributing candles on the feast of the Purification
which is, of course, associated with nursing mothers. *Via
della Curia 2*

## San Luigi dei Francesi (St Louis of the French)

As the name rather indicates, this is the national church
of the French. It is a Renaissance building, commissioned
in 1518 but not completed until 1589. The construction
incorporated a wall of the baths of Nero as restored by

Alexander Severus in AD 227. There is little of interest here for a pilgrim except the canvases of the life of St Matthew by Caravaggio, commissioned c. 1597. *Piazza San Luigi dei Francesi 5 / Via Santa Giovanna d'Arco*

*This splendidly painted wooden pulpit is to be found in the church of San Luigi dei Francesi, St Louis of the French, the French national church in Rome, and dates from the sixteenth century – the period in which the church itself was built.*

## La Maddalena (St Mary Magdalene)

This is entirely a seventeenth-century building, though constructed on the site of an earlier church. The site was acquired by St Camillus de Lellis (1550–1614), a one-time soldier and inveterate gambler, who underwent a conversion and became a priest and a disciple of St Philip Neri. He founded an order, the Priest Ministers of the Sick or Camillians, whose headquarters are here. The remains of the saint are interred in a sarcophagus in the transept, apart from his heart, which is enshrined in a monstrance kept in the chapel of relics. In the chapel of the crucifix is a crucifix which is said to have lowered one arm to embrace St Camillus as he lay dying. As is appropriate for a church in the charge of the Camillians, there is a sixteenth-century icon of Our Lady, known as the Health of the Sick. *Piazza della Maddalena 53*

## *San Marcello al Corso (St Marcellus on the Corso)

Marcellus was Bishop of Rome at the very end of the first decade of the fourth century, though his exact dates are disputed. The legend has it that the church which bears his name was a stable where he was made to serve as a groom by an angry Emperor Maxentius. It is more likely that he was banished from the city by Maxentius after causing division within the Christian community, and that he died away from Rome, though his body was brought back and interred in the cemetery of Santa Priscilla. Whatever the details, a church was in existence by 418. It was several times restored, but in 1519 it was completely destroyed by fire, with only a wooden crucifix remaining which is now venerated in the chapel of the crucifix in what is a sixteenth-century church, with a seventeenth-century façade. The crucifix is sometimes carried in procession through the streets of Rome. The third chapel on the right is perhaps of particular interest to British pilgrims, for it has the tomb of the English Cardinal Weld (1773–1837), who was known as the Cardinal of the Seven Sacraments as he had been married before becoming a priest: his daughter, son-in-law and grandchildren lived with him in Rome. Also buried in the church, down at the far right, is Cardinal Ercole Consalvi (1757–1824), one of the most famous, and able, of Cardinal Secretaries of State. Entombed in the main altar are the relics of St Marcellus. There is an ancient baptistery, perhaps as early as the foundation of the church, which can be accessed through a door in the church, though it is actually under the neighbouring bank, and can also be seen from within the bank. The church serves as the headquarters of the Servite Order. *Piazza di San Marcello 5*

## *Santi Marcellino e Pietro (SS Marcellinus and Peter)

Marcellinus was, apparently, a priest and Peter an exorcist; they were martyred together in Rome in 304. There was a considerable cult of the two in the early Middle Ages, and they are mentioned together in the Roman canon. They were originally buried in the catacomb named after them, but their relics were brought to this church in 1256. The 'titulus' is quite an ancient one, possibly going back to the end of the fourth century, if not earlier, but the building is of the eighteenth century and is of no great interest. The relics of St Marcia, a martyr of whom nothing is known, are beneath the main altar. *Via Merulana 162*

## *San Marco (St Mark's)

This minor basilica near the Piazza Venezia was in all probability founded by Pope St Mark (8 January–16 October 336), about whom almost nothing is known: his relics are in a porphyry urn beneath the high altar. It was later rededicated to St Mark the Evangelist, the patron of Venice. It was the titular church of the Venice-born Cardinal Pietro Barbo, from 1464 to 1471 Pope Paul II. Paul II continued to use it as his official residence after his election, hence the elaborate portico from which he could give his blessing. It was originally built upon a Roman house, possibly that of Mark before he became pope, which would explain the 'titulus'. It was rebuilt in the fifth century and again towards the end of the eighth century. It was flooded in 791 and restored yet again by Pope Gregory IV (827–44) who had a mosaic portrait of himself erected in the apse. The crypt houses the relics of SS Abdon and Sennen, said to be martyrs in Persia in AD 303, but they are more likely to have died in Rome. *Piazza San Marco 48; entrance by way of the Palazzo Venezia*

## Santa Maria ad Martyres (The Pantheon)

This Roman building, often said to be a temple 'to all the gods', was converted to a Christian church between 609 and 613. It was first built by Marcus Agrippa 27–25 BC, but then destroyed in the fire of AD 80 under Nero. It was replaced by Domitian, Emperor 81–96, but then struck by lightning in 110 when it burned down again. It was finally completed by Hadrian about the year 125, quite possibly not as a temple – a cult of 'all the gods' was unknown in Rome – so much as a ceremonial space. It was converted into a church under Pope Boniface IV, which may well account for its survival for nearly two millennia as the building with the largest concrete span of its dome. The dome was originally covered in bronze, but this was removed in 655 and replaced with lead by the Syrian Pope St Gregory III (731–41). The massive bronze doors are ancient, but not original to the building. The dedication to 'Our Lady and All the Martyrs' is sometimes said to be the origin of the feast of All Saints but, although there is an altar directly opposite the entrance with a thirteenth-century icon of the Madonna, the sense is more of a mausoleum than a church: the building contains the tomb of the artist Raphael and of kings Victor Emmanuel II and Umberto I of Italy. *Piazza della Rotonda 12*

*A view at night of the façade of the Pantheon. This first-century Roman temple was turned into a church in the seventh century, with a dedication to Our Lady with the Martyrs (Santa Maria ad Martyres).*

## Santa Maria ai Monti (Our Lady of the Hills)

This is the official name of the church, but it is also known as Santa Maria dei Monti or, more commonly, as Madonna dei Monti and is located in the Via della Madonna dei Monti. This sixteenth-century church was built to house an icon of the Madonna with SS Lawrence and Stephen, found painted on the wall of a barn which stood on this spot. The barn itself was the remains of a thirteenth-century convent of Poor Clares who had moved elsewhere. The icon, which looks fifteenth century, became locally an object of much veneration, all the more so after a blind woman claimed to have been cured through praying before it. Enough money was donated to pay for the church, which was a favourite of St Benedict Joseph Labre (1748–83), the patron saint of tramps. The saint was born near Boulogne but spent much of his life as a poor pilgrim, wandering from shrine to shrine until in 1774 he took up residence in the arches of Rome's Colosseum. He was taken ill in this church and carried to a nearby butcher's shop, where he died. He was buried in Madonna dei Monti. Widely regarded as a saint – if an eccentric one – in his lifetime, he was canonized in 1881. *Via della Madonna dei Monti 41*

## Santa Maria Antiqua (Old St Mary's)

It is not easy to get access to this church, which is subject to regular excavations and is part of the archaeological site of the Forum, for which a ticket is required. It is, in any case, not a likely pilgrimage destination, though it was the original home of the icon which bears its name and which is now in **Santa Francesca Romana**. It is possible, indeed likely, that the building was not originally a church but a guard house, when there was a Byzantine governor

*This small church, known as Santa Maria Antiqua (Old St Mary's), in the Forum dates from the sixth century, though in the middle of the ninth century it was covered over with debris during an earthquake and another church was later built on top of it. It was rediscovered at the end of the nineteenth century.*

of Rome living on the Palatine in the middle of the sixth century, and that it was adapted to be a church soon afterwards, in the late sixth or early seventh century – though it may be earlier. It had to be abandoned in the ninth century, perhaps because of an earthquake in 847 which buried it under the rubble of other collapsed buildings, and worship was transferred to **Santa Maria Nova**. In the twelfth century another church, now disappeared, was built over it and Santa Maria Antiqua was only rediscovered at the very end of the nineteenth century.

Before the earthquake it had been richly decorated with frescoes of Greek as well as Latin saints, all depicted in Byzantine-style dress. These may reflect the earlier Byzantine reconquest of Rome or, more likely, they were painted as a reaction to the iconoclast controversy – the destruction of icons – in the East and were perhaps the work of refugees from iconoclasm. They were painted during the pontificates of John VII (705–07), Zacharias (741–52) and Paul I (757–67), all of whom are represented with square haloes indicating they were still alive: popes Zacharias and Paul I are venerated as saints. Some of the frescoes are in good order, though most have badly deteriorated. *Largo Romolo e Remo 1*

*The fact that Santa Maria Antiqua was covered over for centuries helped to preserve some striking frescoes, including this crucifixion scene, painted in the mid-eighth century.*

## Santa Maria degli Angeli (St Mary of the Angels)

*An odd thing to find in a church. In Santa Maria degli Angeli (Our Lady of the Angels) there was placed, at the very beginning of the eighteenth century, this meridian line along which, through a hole in the wall, the sun would shine at noon, solar time, thereby setting the clock for the Romans.*

This is one of the more unusual of Roman churches, in that it was built within, and incorporates some of the ruins of, the Baths of Diocletian. These had, by the sixteenth century, become overgrown and were used as a hunting ground by

Rome's nobility. A priest with a devotion to the archangels persuaded Pope Pius IV (1559–65) to launch the project, using a ground plan produced by Michelangelo. One enters the church across what would have been, in the baths, the frigidarium or cool bath, continuing on to the calidarium or hot bath. An oddity within the church, installed in 1703, is the line of Rome's meridian, along which the sun shines at 12.15 pm each day, or an hour later during summer time (Rome is at latitude 15).

For a pilgrim there are two things of interest. The chapel of the martyrs on the left of the presbyterium has the supposed relics of Saturninus, Cyriac, Largus, Smaragdus, Sisinnius, Trasonius and Pope Marcellinus, who had all died, it was believed, while they were being used as slave labour to build the baths. There are also the relics of many other unknown martyrs who similarly perished: the full title of the church is Our Lady of the Angels and of the Martyrs. Cardinal Camillo Cybo (1681–1743), who built the chapel of the relics, also donated relics of the four great Doctors of the Western Church, SS Jerome, Ambrose, Augustine and Gregory. In the apse there is a painting, sometimes attributed to Lorenzo Lotto (c. 1480–1556), entitled 'The Virgin Mary on the Throne between Seven Angels', which shows her being crowned by the Archangels Michael and Gabriel. She is suckling the Christ Child: hence the painting is known as 'The Madonna of the Milk'. When it was first opened the church was given to the Carthusians, and the remains of their monastery can still be seen: visiting the Museo Nazionale delle Terme – an archaeological museum which has also been carved out of the Baths of Diocletian – allows the visitor to see the monastery's cloister. Incidentally, the church has a famous organ and a strong musical tradition, and its cavernous interior is often used for concerts and similar events, as well as state funerals.
*Via Cernale 9 (Piazza della Repubblica)*

# Santa Maria dei Miracoli (St Mary of the Miracles)

*The twin churches of Santa Maria dei Miracoli (Our Lady of Miracles, right) with Santa Maria in Montesanto (Our Lady of Montesanto, left) mark the entrance to Rome at the end of the Via Flaminia, the main route into the city for pilgrims.*

The origins of the present church are similar to those of its 'twin' on the Piazza del Popolo, **Santa Maria in Montesanto**. They both marked the point where pilgrims entered Rome at the end of the Via Flaminia, passing through the Porta del Popolo. Pope Alexander VII (1655–67) ordered their construction to create a suitable architectural greeting to those arriving. In the case of this church, however, there had been an earlier chapel which housed the icon of the Madonna from which it takes its name. According to the story, a woman who had dropped her baby into the Tiber ran to this icon, then attached to the Porta del Popolo. The baby was saved, which led to the great veneration of the image, so great that a chapel was constructed next to the river to house it. Because the chapel was subject to regular floods, the icon was moved to what is now San Giacomo in Augusta and replaced by a copy. The chapel was demolished on the orders of Pope Alexander to make way for this new church, where the miraculous icon hangs over the altar. The church is in the charge of the Fathers of the Society of the Sacred Heart of Jesus of Bétharram, whose founder, St Michael Garicoïts (1797–1863), is represented by a statue in the first chapel on the right. Under the altar of the first chapel on the left are the relics of St Candida, of whom nothing is known, brought from the catacomb of St Priscilla. *Via del Corso 528 / Piazza del Popolo*

## Santa Maria del Pianto (Our Lady of Tears)

The story goes that in 1546 two men were arguing in front of an image of the Madonna. They drew daggers, but one appealed for mercy whereupon the other dropped his weapon. Then the one who had made the appeal stabbed his now unarmed opponent to death. At this the icon, a fifteenth-century fresco, was seen to shed tears and was subsequently brought into a nearby church, up to that point called San Salvatore, which dated from at least the twelfth century. It was in a dilapidated state and was rebuilt in the seventeenth century, though the rebuilding was never wholly completed. Nonetheless there is a fine high altar in which this image is enshrined. The church is administered by the Oblates of the Virgin Mary, a religious order founded by the Venerable Bruno Lanteri (1759–1830) which came officially into existence in 1826. The fathers and brothers give retreats and parish missions. They do not seem to have a presence in the British Isles, though they flourish in the Americas and elsewhere. *Via Santa Maria dei Calderari 20*

# Santa Maria del Popolo (Our Lady of the People)

*The church of Santa Maria del Popolo (Our Lady of the People) was built from 1471 to 1484 and is a fine example of Italian Renaissance architecture. It houses the much venerated icon of the same name, enshrined above the high altar.*

One of the most popular churches in Rome, the traditional story of its foundation is that it was built on the site of the tomb of Nero by Pope Paschal II in 1099 to exorcize his spirit – his remains were deposited in the Tiber. The church was enlarged and consecrated in 1235 by Pope Gregory IX who gave it an icon of the Virgin – the Madonna del Popolo, said to have been painted by St Luke – which had hitherto been venerated in St John Lateran. The icon, which stylistically is from the twelfth or thirteenth century, is over the main altar. The church was rebuilt by Pope Sixtus IV between 1472 and 1478, making it one of the earliest

Renaissance churches in Rome. It is full of monuments to the great and (not always so) good of the city, including Giovanni Borgia, the son of Pope Alexander VI, and his mother the Pope's mistress Vannozza dei Cattanei: they are buried in the Cicada chapel in the transept. In the sacristy is an altar and tabernacle made for Cardinal Rodrigo Borgia before his election to the papacy. There are many tombs of cardinals, especially of the della Rovere family. In a chapel to the left of the main altar are two canvases by Caravaggio, the 'Conversion of St Paul' and the 'Execution of St Peter' painted in 1602: Peter and Paul being jointly regarded as the founders of the Christian community in Rome even though there were Christians in the city when they arrived. There was a further restoration during the pontificate of the Chigi Pope Alexander VII (1655–67) who when still a cardinal also completed the Chigi chapel, in effect almost a small church in its own right. It had been begun by the banker Agostino Chigi to a design by Raphael, and Agostino and his brother are buried there. The church is in the care of the Augustinian Friars, and it was in this community that Martin Luther lived during his visit to Rome in 1511. *Piazza del Popolo 12*

## Santa Maria del Rosario a Monte Mario
(Our Lady of the Rosary on Monte Mario)

This church is part of a convent of Dominican nuns, the descendants of the community which originally was housed in **San Sisto**. Perhaps because of its location, the church is not mentioned in most of the guidebooks. It dates from the seventeenth century and has had a troubled history: the Dominicans came here as recently as 1931 from **Santi Domenico e Sisto** bringing with them, apparently, a collection of relics, including some of St Dominic. They also brought with them the Madonna of St Luke, which is now housed in the church. It is yet another icon purporting to have been painted by St Luke, and it is of considerable age, possibly arriving in Rome in the fifth century, though the first firm date is the early years of the tenth century. It is now dated to the seventh or eighth century and was painted in the Middle East. It can be found to the left of the sanctuary. *Via Trionfale 175*


## Santa Maria dell'Anima

(St Mary of the Souls [in Purgatory])

This is the German national church in Rome, though its origins lie in a hospice for pilgrims founded by a Dutch couple c. 1350. The hospice was a success, and moved to this site in 1386. The hospice, which served pilgrims from the Holy Roman Empire of which what is now Holland was a part, had a chapel which in 1431 was converted into the present church. It served both Germans and Dutch until the outbreak of World War II. Inside the church is the tomb of the short-lived Pope Adrian VI (1522–23) who came from Utrecht and was the last non-Italian Bishop of Rome until the election of John Paul II in 1978. Above the main door is an image of the Virgin Mary with two souls in purgatory. This is a copy: the original is kept in the sacristy. The church is rarely open except for (a German-language) mass on Sundays. *Via Santa Maria dell'Anima 64*


## Santa Maria dell'Archetto (Our Lady of the Bow)

The name is a bit of a puzzle as 'archetto' usually means 'bow' as in the instrument used for playing a violin but it could also mean 'little arch', which would be appropriate:

the church was created in an alleyway called Vicolo dell'Archetto. The alleyway was crossed by an arch leading between two buildings. In the alleyway was displayed a painting on a large tile of Mary the Mother of Jesus as a young girl. The painting, completed in 1691, was apparently placed on the outside wall of a building, something that was commonly done. Shortly after it was erected the image was seen to move its eyes. This obviously attracted pilgrims and the painting was moved to a spot under the arch. Then the vicolo was blocked off at both ends and finally, in the mid-nineteenth century, this very small church was constructed in the alleyway. The painting came to be known as Mary, Cause of Our Joy, one of the invocations from the Litany of Loreto. *Via di San Marcello 41*

## Santa Maria della Concezione
(Our Lady of the Conception)

Although this seventeenth-century church contains the shrine of St Felix of Cantalice, it is best known, and most visited, because of its ossuary. St Felix (d. 1587) was a Capuchin lay brother – the church is in the charge of the Capuchin branch of the Franciscans – from Cantalice in the Abruzzi, who begged alms for his Order in the streets of Rome and taught catechism to children. He is entombed beneath the altar of the second chapel on the left-hand side. In the first chapel on the right is a painting by Guido Reni, 'St Michael Trampling the Devil', in which the devil's face is supposedly that of Pope Leo X. The relics under the main altar are claimed to be those of Justin Martyr (c. 100–65), a convert to Christianity c. 130 and the first Christian philosopher. Though he came from Samaria he taught in Rome, and was executed there under Marcus Aurelius. In the museum is the painting 'St Francis at Prayer', now firmly attributed to Caravaggio. The ossuary, entered through the museum, is decorated, if that is the word, with the bones of people, particularly but not only the friars, who had originally been buried in the crypt, which contains soil especially imported from the Holy Land. Some of the skeletal remains had been brought from an earlier Capuchin house in Rome. Part of the convent has been turned into a hotel, I Cappucini. *Via Veneto 27*

## Santa Maria della Consolazione
(Our Lady of Consolation)

The story of this church, built to house an icon of Our Lady of Consolation, is complex. A nobleman, imprisoned on the Campidoglio in 1385, left money for a picture of Our Lady to be painted on a wall where it might be seen by those awaiting execution. When, some 80 years later, a young man survived hanging because he had been held up, he claimed, by an invisible hand, this apparent miracle was attributed to the painting: the man said he heard the words 'Go, you are consoled' – hence the name of the icon. Devotion to it grew considerably and a church was immediately built to house it. With donations received from devotees a hospital was built on the site, and towards the end of the sixteenth century a new church was erected. A number of saints worked as volunteers in the hospital, including the Jesuits Ignatius Loyola and Aloysius Gonzaga, the latter dying of plague contracted from the patients he attended there.

The hospital took over the nearby Santa Maria delle Grazie, and when this church was closed, its icon of Our Lady was moved to Santa Maria della Consolazione. A copy of the icon of Our Lady from Santa Maria in Portico, which had been moved to **Santa Maria in Campitelli**, was

*According to tradition, the icon above the high
altar was painted, in 1385, so that it might be seen
as a consolation – hence the name, Our Lady of
Consolation – by prisoners about to be executed.*

also placed in the church. The original icon of Santa Maria
della Consolazione is now above the main altar while to
the right of the sanctuary is the shrine of Santa Maria delle
Grazie. The icon here is a twelfth-century copy of the one
which was stolen in 1960. The original was one of several
claimed to have been painted during Mary's lifetime by the
prolific St Luke the Evangelist, and may possibly have been
given by the Emperor to Pope Vitalian in 657. A church
was built for it, and when people living near the church
seemed to escape a plague a few years later, the icon gained

a reputation as miraculous. This was further strengthened by its surviving in the ashes when the church was burnt down (by the Normans) in 1084. It remained in its new home until 1876. *Piazza della Consolazione 94*

*So many people came to see the icon of Our Lady of Consolation, and left offerings, that a hospital was built behind the church. The apse can be seen to the right of the picture, the hospital to the left. This was only for men. There was a separate hospital for women across the road.*

## Santa Maria della Luce (Our Lady of Light)

In 1730 a young man about to commit suicide saw the image of Our Lady displayed on a wall, and determined to stay alive. Shortly afterwards a blind man had his sight restored after praying to this same image (hence the name, 'Our Lady of Light'). Subsequently this icon was trans-

*In 1730 the sight of this image, known as
Our Lady of Light, reputedly heartened a
young man about to commit suicide, and
shortly afterwards restored the sight of a
blind man. The icon was then transferred to
a nearby church which was named after it,
Santa Maria della Luce.*

ferred to the nearby church of San Salvatore in Corte which
had been entrusted two years earlier to the Minim Friars.
As a consequence of the devotion to the icon the friars
were able to rebuild the church, and it came to be known
under the above title: its earlier name remains something
of a puzzle. There is a tradition that it was founded in

the third or fourth century, though the earliest definite evidence of its existence comes only from the late tenth century. It is now in the charge of the Missionaries of St Charles Borromeo, known as Scalabrinians, founded by Bishop Giovanni Battista Scalabrini in Piacenza in 1887. Their primary purpose was to care for Italian migrants from Latin America, and the church is a centre of pastoral care for Latin Americans. The icon of Our Lady of Light is enthroned above the main altar. *Via della Luce / Via della Lungaretta 22A*

## Santa Maria della Pace (Our Lady of Peace)

The very constricted site determined the unusual shape of this church's interior. It replaced a chapel of the water-carriers, the men who brought water from the Tiber to those parts of the city not served by other sources, and in the earlier chapel, dedicated to St Andrew, hung a picture of the Madonna and Child. When a soldier struck the image of the Virgin her breast began to bleed, so the story goes. Sixtus IV (1471–84) visited the image during the war between the Papal States and Florence (1478–80), and vowed to build a church in thanksgiving for peace which was largely his doing. The picture now hangs over the main altar. The church was much restored in the baroque style by Alexander VII (1655–67). In the first chapel to the right – built by a renowned banker and ancestor of Pope Alexander – there are frescoes by Raphael. The cloister was designed by Bramante, and added in 1504. *Piazza Santa Maria della Pace / Vicolo del Arco della Pace 5*

## Santa Maria della Scala (Our Lady of the Staircase)

*This sixteenth-century fresco, known as Our*
*Lady of the Staircase (Santa Maria della Scala),*
*had originally been painted on a staircase on*
*the outside of a house, but after devotion to*
*it increased it was moved to the church which*
*was constructed to house it.*

This is one of several Roman churches built to house
an icon, in this instance one that had been placed on an
outside staircase to a house and which, it was claimed,
had cured a deformed child, thus leading to a cult of the
image. The church which houses it was built in the last

decade of the sixteenth century, and the first decade of the seventeenth. The fresco is now to be found in the transept on the left of the church. Responsibility for the church was given from the beginning to the Discalced (shoeless) Carmelites – a community of whom is still there – with the result that much of the iconography reflects the history of the Carmelites. There is a relic of the right foot of St Teresa of Avila in the right transept. *Piazza della Scala 23*

## Santa Maria della Vittoria (Our Lady of Victory)

This superbly decorated church – for aficionados of baroque – was built by the Discalced Carmelite Friars between 1608 and 1626 though the attached convent (only a small section still occupied by the friars) opened in 1612. It was erected in place of a small hermitage dedicated to St Paul, and St Paul was also the first dedication of the church. In 1620, however, during the Battle of the White Mountain in which Catholic imperial troops overcame a Protestant Czech army, thus preserving the Catholicism of Bohemia, the Discalced friar who was chaplain to the imperial forces wore around his neck an icon of the Nativity. This was brought to Rome and installed in the church, which then became Our Lady of Victory. Unfortunately the original icon was destroyed in a fire in 1833, and that now on display above the high altar is a copy. The story of the icon and of the battle is represented in some of the decoration of the church. Visitors are attracted to the church, however, by the famous statue by Bernini of St Teresa of Avila in ecstasy which is housed in a chapel also designed by Bernini. St Teresa (1515–82), a Doctor of the Church, was the founder of the Discalced Carmelites. *Via XX Settembre 17*

## Santa Maria di Loreto (Our Lady of Loreto)

The original church on this site was the guild chapel of the confraternity of bakers, and it proved too small. It was therefore demolished and this church was built in its place at the beginning of the sixteenth century. It is notable for its shrine to St Expeditus. His statue holds a cross inscribed 'Hodie' ('today') and is trampling on 'Cras' ('tomorrow'). The name may be mistaken or, alternatively, 'expeditus' was a lightly armed Roman soldier – and he is portrayed as a soldier in the iconography. He is listed quite early on as a martyr in Armenia, but his cult grew after a parcel of relics, marked 'expedite' (urgent) arrived at a convent. The nun opening it mistook it for the name of the saint and the nuns prayed to him – apparently successfully. This may, however, very well be a Catholic urban myth. He is not listed in the Roman Martyrology. *Piazza Madonna di Loreto 26*

## Santa Maria in Aracoeli
(St Mary at the Altar of Heaven)

At the top of over 120 steps – there is an easier way from the Piazza del Campidoglio to the right of the Capitoline Museum – this church used to be called Santa Maria in Capitolio (on the Capitoline Hill), and was the site of a Byzantine-rite monastery, built on the site of a Roman temple to Juno Moneta where there had been a Roman mint. The monastery is first mentioned in 547, but was certainly there earlier. In the ninth century it became a Benedictine house, and in the thirteenth a Franciscan friary. Little remains of the friary, largely destroyed to make way for the monument to Victor Emanuel which dominates the Piazza Venezia. The change of name to Aracoeli reflects a medieval legend that the Emperor Augustus saw the Virgin Mary in a vision standing on an altar, with the child Jesus in her arms. It is claimed that the altar Augustus saw is that now in the transept on which stands a porphyry urn containing the alleged remains of St Helena, the mother of the Emperor Constantine.

There are a number of memorials to saintly members of the Franciscan Order, in particular Pinturicchio's frescoes of the life of St Bernardino of Siena – who popularized the devotion to the Holy Name – in the chapel to the right of the main door, and beyond that, in the chapel of St Jerome, is a sixteenth-century fresco of famous Franciscan scholars including the Blessed John Duns Scotus. The chapel of San Diego is dedicated to the Franciscan saint Diego de San Nicolás after whom San Diego in California is named. In the chapel of St Francis are entombed the remains of Brother Juniper, one of the companions of the saint of Assisi. Behind the high altar is an icon of the Virgin painted on beechwood. It is probably from the tenth century though may very well be earlier, and legend has it that it was the icon carried through the streets of Rome by Pope St Gregory I (the Great, 590–604) to defend the populace from plague, a scene depicted in the right ambo of the transept. The icon was certainly carried through the streets in 1348 to protect the city from the Black Death.

For Romans, however, perhaps the most significant sight in the church is the Bambino ('Christ-child'), a figure of a baby said to have been carved in the Holy Land by a Franciscan from an olive tree in the Garden of Gethsemane and brought to Rome in the mid-seventeenth century. Many cures were attributed to the statue, and it was frequently carried from the church to visit a sick or dying person at home or in hospital: the Bambino had its own coach to take it around the city. At Christmas it is placed in an elaborate crib in the chapel of the Nativity and much venerated: children even write letters to it, as they do to Father Christmas. The original was encrusted with jewels from grateful beneficiaries of its healing powers or from other devotees, but it was stolen in 1994 and has never been recovered. The Bambino there now is a replacement which has not attracted the same devotion.

The church's magnificent gilded ceiling commemorates the victory of the Christian fleet over the Ottomans at the battle of Lepanto in 1571. The papal admiral, Marcantonio Colonna, was received in triumph on his return to Rome, and the procession terminated in Santa Maria in Aracoeli, the church of the city of Rome. *Piazza del Campidoglio 4*

## Santa Maria in Campitelli (St Mary in Campitelli)

Sometimes known as Santa Maria del Portico, this church perhaps dates from the fifteenth century as a chapel of **Santa Maria in Aracoeli.** Beneath it lies the temple of Jupiter Stator, one of the 'victory temples' which marked the starting points for Roman triumphs. The church became an independent parish only in 1618, when it was given to the Clerks Regular of the Mother of God who still serve the church, and whose headquarters are beside it. The alternative name comes from the icon of the Madonna which has been enshrined there since the twelfth century, though the icon in the Byzantine style is certainly older. How much older is disputed, the church itself claiming that there are enough stylistic aspects to suggest it goes back to the sixth century. It is said to represent the vision of St Galla, a pious woman who spent her life serving the poor, and that the icon was carried in procession by Pope St Gregory the Great (590–604) to protect the city against plague.

Architecturally the church is unlike any other in Rome, the ground plan being in the form of two crosses, the first

*The 'Gloria' above the main altar of Santa
Maria in Campitelli was built the year
after Bernini's 'Gloria' in St Peter's. It was
created to house the icon of Santa Maria del
Portico, supposedly a sixth-century image
but more likely to date from somewhat later.*

on entry with equal lengths, the second beyond in the
cupola a more conventional shape. The second chapel on
the left is dedicated to the founder of the Clerks Regular
with a relic. John (Giovanni) Leonardi (c. 1541–1609)
was born in Lucca – the full name of his order is 'Clerks
Regular of the Mother of God of Lucca' – where for a time
he worked as a pharmacist before becoming a priest. As

a priest he was a zealous opponent of Protestantism and founded the Confraternity of Christian Doctrine to prepare laymen to teach the Catholic faith. He also helped create the Collegio Urbano which trains missionary priests. He died in Rome and was canonized in 1938. In the sacristy is an altar which is said to have belonged to the theologian St Gregory of Nazianzen (c. 329–89). Santa Maria in Campitelli was the titular church of Henry Stuart, Cardinal Duke of York (1725–1807), the younger brother of Bonnie Prince Charlie and, as 'King Henry IX', the last direct Stuart claimant to the English throne. Since his time the church has been a centre of prayer for the conversion of England to Catholicism. *Piazza di Campitelli 9*

*The shrine of St John Leonardi (San Giovanni Leonardi, 1541–1609) in the church of Santa Maria in Campitelli. St John was the founder of the Clerks Regular of the Mother of God of Lucca – Lucca was where the saint was born, and where he founded his Congregation.*

## Santa Maria in Campo Marzio
(St Mary in Campo Marzio)

The original dedication of this church, formerly a Benedictine convent, was to Our Lady and St Gregory of Nazianzen. The relics of St Gregory (c. 329–89), who was one of the Doctors of the Eastern Church, were brought here from Constantinople, presumably during the iconoclasm controversy, and were buried in an associated church, still dedicated to him but inaccessible. In any case the saint's relics were moved to St Peter's in 1580. Though the church is an ancient one, dating from at least the early years of the tenth century, it was rebuilt in the seventeenth century. The nuns were driven out in 1873 and their nunnery is now office accommodation for the Italian parliament. The church has since become the national church of Syrian-rite (Syro-Antiochene) Catholics who are in full communion with Rome. *Piazza Campo Marzio 45*

## Santa Maria in Cosmedin (Our Lady of Beauty)

As noted in the Glossary, Cosmedin comes from the Greek word meaning 'ornate', hence the translation, but it may also be derived from the name of a monastery just outside the walls of Constantinople. This church was rebuilt in 782 to serve the needs of Greek monks who had fled to Rome at the time of the iconoclast Isaurian emperors – though the 780s would have been an odd time to flee because the first period of iconoclasm was coming to an end. Rather appropriately, the church now serves the needs of Rome's Melkite (Byzantine-rite) community. It is located at what was the easiest point to cross the Tiber, and there may have been a market, possibly for cattle, in this area which would have made its origins, probably in the fourth century, as

*The façade of Santa Maria in Cosmedin was constructed at the very end of the nineteenth century in what was thought to be a medieval style. The splendid and particularly tall campanile is, however, authentically medieval.*

a deaconry serving the needs of the poor of the Christian community all the more understandable.

One of the cardinal deacons who held the title of Santa Maria in Cosmedin was the English Reginald Pole (1500–58), the last archbishop of Canterbury to have been in communion with Rome. In the thirteenth century care of the church was taken over by secular canons who established themselves in the adjoining convent. One who lived there was St John Baptist de Rossi (1698–1764) who was renowned for his concern for the poor of Rome. He operated out of the church of Santissima Trinità dei Pellegrini (a sixteenth-century church with a pilgrims' hospice attached, the latter no longer surviving), and this is where he was buried. His tomb was moved in 1965 to a church dedicated in his memory. There is a chapel in his memory within Santa Maria in Cosmedin where is kept the skull of St Valentine, supposedly the Valentine celebrated on 14 February as the patron saint of romance. Next to nothing is known of St Valentine, but he is thought to have been the bishop of Terni who was martyred on the Via Flaminia – at least, that is the entry in the Roman Martyrology for 14 February.

*The alleged skull of St Valentine is kept on the altar dedicated to St John Baptist de Rossi and on 14 February, his feast day, is taken from the reliquary and crowned.*

The interior of the church is interesting, and there are the remains of what may have been a fourth-century BC altar to Hercules in the crypt. Most visitors to the church, however, come to see a pre-Christian disc, the Bocca della Verità ('mouth of truth'), which is mounted on a column to the left of the entrance. It is not at all clear what this figure of a man's head with a wide-open mouth may originally have been: possibly a mouthpiece for an oracle or a fountain. It was certainly something of considerable value, probably dating from the first century BC. The story is that anyone who puts his or her hand into the mouth and tells a lie will have the fingers bitten off. It gives its name to the piazza in which the church stands. *Piazza Bocca della Verità*

## *Santa Maria in Domnica (Our Lady's Church)

The meaning of the name of this minor basilica is uncertain. One suggestion is that it is a corruption of 'dominicum', a word in early Christian usage for church ('dominica' is Christian usage for Sunday, 'the Lord's day'). The church was in existence by the end of the eighth century, but midway through the ninth century it was restored by Pope Paschal I (817–24) who is depicted in a contemporary mosaic kneeling in front of the Madonna, holding her shoe. This is the first known example of the Madonna taking pride of place in a church – though of course Christ is there also.

The church was built on the foundations of a Roman fire and police station, which can be glimpsed in the crypt. An alternative name for this basilica is Santa Maria alla Navicella ('little boat'). The boat in question, a sculpture, now stands outside the church and gives its name to the street. It is also of unknown origin. There are no notable relics in the church, but visitors from Bavaria and

Luxembourg might be interested in the tomb of Anna of Luxembourg, who died in 1954. She was princess of the house of Luxembourg who married into the ducal family of Bavaria, and was the last crowned princess of Bavaria. The parish clergy are members of the recently founded (1985) Priestly Fraternity of the Missionaries of St Charles Borromeo. *Piazza Navicella 10*

## Santa Maria in Monserrato degli Spagnoli
(Our Lady of Monserrat of the Spaniards)

It really ought to be 'of the Catalans' because its icon-ography reflects that region of Spain, although it is now the national church in Rome for all Spaniards. While there is nothing in this basically sixteenth-century building a pil-grim might wish to venerate, it has been included because the two Borgia (Borja in Spanish) popes are interred here, Callistus III (1455–58) and the notorious Alexander VI (1492–1503). *Via de Monserrato / Via Giulia 151*

## Santa Maria in Montesanto (St Mary in Montesanto)

This minor basilica was built – together with **Santa Maria dei Miracoli** – on the Piazza del Popolo which marked the point where pilgrims entered Rome at the end of the Via Flaminia, passing through the Porta del Popolo. Pope Alexander VII (1655–67) ordered their construction to create a suitable architectural greeting to those arriving. This church was given to a branch of the Carmelite Order (they are no longer there) which had begun life near Messina at a place called Monte Santo, hence the name of this church. An icon of Our Lady of Monte Santo had been much venerated in Messina and a copy that was brought here can still be seen over the high altar. The parish has a particular outreach to the artists who gathered in the neighbourhood, and still celebrates an 'artists' mass'. *Via del Babuino 197*

## Santa Maria in Monticelli (St Mary in Monticelli)

The present church, though much remodelled in the eighteenth and nineteenth centuries, was consecrated by Pope Paschal II (1099–1118) in 1101. The campanile is obviously Romanesque. Inside there are remains of a twelfth-century mosaic depicting the face of Christ which, it is thought, was given to the church at its consecration by Pope Paschal. More particularly, there is a fourteenth-century crucifix, which is known to have been venerated by St Bridget of Sweden. The church houses the alleged relics of martyrs named Nympha, Maximilian, Eustace and Quodvultdeus, brought there by Pope Urban III (1185–87). They were unknown, but because there was some suggestion that Maximilian had been bishop of Palermo, they became known collectively as the martyrs of Palermo. *Via di Santa Maria in Monticelli 28*

## Santa Maria in Traspontina
(St Mary's Across the Bridge)

The bridge mentioned in the name is Ponte Sant'Angelo, that which crosses the Tiber beside Castel Sant'Angelo. Though there had been a medieval – possibly even earlier – church, this was demolished when the defences of the Castel were strengthened, and the present church was begun in the mid-sixteenth century. The church has long been in the care of (Calced) Carmelites, and the dedication is to Our Lady of Mount Carmel. Within the church there is a nineteenth-century statue of Our Lady of Mount Carmel which is the object of much devotion by the parishioners – the church serves the Borgo. In the chapel of SS Peter and Paul are two pillars, claimed to be those to which the saints were tied when they were flogged before their execution. Rather unexpectedly there is in the church a chapel to St Canute, King of Denmark, martyred 1086 in Odense. He was the nephew of the King Canute who ruled England in the early eleventh century, and he twice invaded England in vain attempts to win back the throne. He was murdered in the church of St Alban in Odense, and his body lies there. The presence of this chapel has made Santa Maria in Traspontina the national church in Rome for Danes. *Via della Conciliazione 14*

## *Santa Maria in Trastevere (St Mary in Trastevere)

As is remarked in the Glossary, three of the 'tituli', San Crisogono, San Callisto and Santa Cecilia, were located very close together in Trastevere. The 'titulus' of St Callistus, however, was replaced by that of Santa Maria in Trastevere, which, like the Basilica of the Twelve Apostles, was originally known as the Basilica Julia or the 'titulus' Julii, having in all probability been established by Pope Julius I (337–52). The dedication to Our Lady dates from the pontificate of Adrian I (or Hadrian, 772–95) who restored the church. Gregory IV (827–44) reorganized it and constructed the 'confessio' under the altar to receive the relics of martyrs which, as elsewhere, were in the eighth century brought into the city from their original burial places in the countryside because of the lawlessness outside the city walls. The relics enshrined here are those of two popes, St Callistus I (217–22) and St Cornelius (251–53),

*The portico in front of Santa Maria in Trastevere (St Mary in Trastevere, literally 'across the Tiber') was added in 1702. The statues represent three saints whose relics are interred under the high altar, the martyr Popes Callistus (217–22) and Cornelius (251–53) and, at the far right, the priest Calepodius who was a contemporary of Callistus; the other statue is that of Pope St Julius I (337–52), not a martyr but who is recorded as having founded the church.*

and of the priest Calepodius, who was martyred in 232. Both Callistus and Calepodius have catacombs named after them, of which that of Callistus is the more important.

There was a major rebuilding under Pope Innocent II (1138–48) and much restoration since, especially under Pope Pius IX (1846–78), this last not on the whole being regarded favourably. Despite this, it is one of Rome's most attractive basilicas, resplendent with twelfth- and thirteenth-century mosaics, both on the façade and in the apse (in the apse the upper ones are twelfth century and the lower ones from the thirteenth) and, in contrast to the

*The church of Santa Maria in Trastevere was rebuilt in the twelfth century when, it is believed, this mosaic was added, though it may have been renewed a century later. It depicts the Madonna and Child surrounded either by attendants or, more likely, by the wise and foolish virgins. The much faded frescoes are nineteenth century, ordered by Blessed Pope Pius IX (1846–78), who can just be made out kneeling to the left of Christ.*

bustling piazza outside, extraordinarily peaceful. The relics of the saints already mentioned cannot, unfortunately, be reached, but in a niche at the end of the right aisle there are displayed some chains, said to have bound martyrs on their way to execution, a marble ball which, it is claimed, was tied to St Callistus when he was thrown down the well (the well is nearby, but inaccessible) and some red and black pieces of marble which were simply Roman-standard weights by which quantities might be measured. These were, in antiquity, kept in temples and later in churches.

*The mosaic in the apse of Santa Maria in Trastevere is thought to be contemporary with the building of the church. It depicts Christ in glory with the Madonna on his right and St Peter on his left, surrounded by popes. Pope Innocent II (1130–43), who is credited with rebuilding the church, is on the far left. The frieze beneath shows Christ as the Lamb of God, surrounded by his apostles, represented as sheep.*

In the chapel now reserved for private prayer there is an icon known as the Madonna di Strada Cupa (Our Lady of the Street called Cupa). The street, on the Janiculum, has disappeared: the icon used to stand above the entrance to a vineyard and was moved to the church when, in the early seventeenth century, it became the object of a cult, and was famous for miracles. The chapel was renovated by Henry Stuart, Cardinal Duke of York, who thought of himself, after the death of his brother Bonnie Prince Charlie, as the rightful King of England. He placed the royal arms over the chapel entrance.

On the opposite side of the basilica, in what is known as the Altemps chapel after the Cardinal Altemps who had it built as a memorial to the sixteenth-century Council of Trent (there is a remarkable fresco of the Council), is the icon of the Madonna della Clemenza (Our Lady of Mercy). This dates at least from the eighth century and may even be considerably older, possibly the oldest icon representing Our Lady anywhere, and certainly the oldest in Rome. It has been suggested that the dedication of the basilica to Our Lady may have been made when the icon was placed there: previously it had been dedicated to St Callistus. In the sacristy is a relic of Pope St Urban I (222–30), the gift of the Cardinal Duke of York. There is a further icon of Our Lady to be found in the church, but it is a modern copy of the one venerated at the **Santuario della Madonna del Divino Amore**. Although Santa Maria in Trastevere is not counted as one of the major basilicas, nor was it one of the seven great pilgrim churches, there is at the entrance a Holy Door for use in jubilee years. It often happened in the Middle Ages that the area around **San Paolo fuori le Mura** was flooded, in which case the pilgrims were re-directed to Santa Maria. It is perhaps worth remarking that the Community of San Aegidio, well known for its work for the poor and for international peace-making, has its headquarters next to this church, and uses it for worship. *Via della Paglia 14C / Piazza Santa Maria in Trastevere*

## Santa Maria in Trivio (Our Lady at the Crossroads)

The name means 'at the junction of three roads', which is a fair description of its location. The origin of the church is intriguing. It was constructed not as a church but as a hospice for pilgrims to Rome by Belisarius, the general tasked with recovering Italy from the Ostrogoths and bringing it back into subjection to the Emperor in Constantinople. By the early Middle Ages the hospice had become a church, and the medieval church was completely rebuilt towards the end of the sixteenth century. A number of different religious orders have been given responsibility for the church, but Pius IX put it in the charge of the Congregation of the Missionaries of the Precious Blood who undertake to do whatever work in the Church seems most needed. It was founded in 1815 by St Gaspare del Bufalo (1786–1837) whose shrine is to be found within the church, as is the shrine to Giovanni Merlini (1795–1873) who was St Gaspare's successor-but-one as head of the Congregation and whose cause for canonization has been introduced. *Piazza dei Crociferi 49*

## Santa Maria in Via (Our Lady in the Street)

The origins of this church are unclear, but it was in existence by the tenth century. As it presently exists, however, it dates from the sixteenth century and is served by priests of the Servite (Servants of Mary) Order, a fact which accounts for much of the iconography. It is of particular interest because of an event which occurred on 26 September 1256. During the night a well serving a stable yard next to the medieval building overflowed. In the water and floating (that was the particularly miraculous aspect) was a tile with an image of the Madonna on it. A chapel was built round the well, with the icon becoming the altarpiece under the title of 'Our Lady of the Well'. The water is drinkable, and a Servite friar is likely to offer visitors a glass. One account of this church warns that the water may be toxic to non-believers! St Robert Bellarmine (1542–1621), a Jesuit theologian and a cardinal, held the title of Santa Maria in Via, and a chair which he used can still be seen in the sacristy. *Via del Mortaro 24 (Largo Chigi)*

## *Santa Maria in Via Lata
(Our Lady on the Via Lata [the Corso])

In his *The Christian's Guide to Rome*, Canon Stanley Luff describes this minor basilica as having 'a hazy history'. As it stands, it is basically a seventeenth-century building, but it was erected on the site of what may have been an 'insula' or block of flats, which would have had business premises on the ground floor. Originally this church was a deaconry, a place from which welfare was distributed, and there is evidence that part of the crypt was a storehouse. The crypt has frescoes which date from the eighth century or even earlier, and part of it was adapted as a chapel. Legend has it that it was in these rooms that St Paul lodged, and St Luke the Evangelist was here too. There is a well which, again according to legend, sprang up miraculously so that St Peter could have water to administer baptism. Beneath the altar in the main church are interred the relics of the martyr St Agapitus, of whom little or nothing is known but who enjoyed a considerable cult in the early church. Above the altar is a twelfth-century icon of Our Lady under the title of 'the Advocate', and which is much venerated, being regarded as miraculous. *Via del Corso 306*

## Santa Maria Maddalena in Campo Marzio *see* La Maddalena

## Santa Maria Nova see Santa Francesca Romana

## Santa Maria Scala Coeli (Our Lady Stairway to Heaven)

This is the church attached to the monastery of **Santi Vincenzo e Anastasio alle Tre Fontane**. The name comes from a supposed vision of St Bernard of Clairvaux (c. 1090–1153), the founder of the Cistercians. While saying mass in what was then a chapel on this site he saw souls being released from purgatory and making their way up to heaven. The chapel was dedicated to Mary, hence the name. It was rebuilt in the 1580s. It has long been a pilgrimage church not because of St Bernard's vision but because in what has become the crypt is a room, which can be visited, where St Paul is said to have been imprisoned before his execution. *Via Laurentina 473*

## Santa Maria sopra Minerva

The name of this church is a puzzle. It is often suggested that the 'sopra Minerva' means that it was built over the temple of Minerva, the Roman goddess of wisdom, but this is not archaeologically correct. The church seems to have been in existence in the eighth century. In the mid-thirteenth century it was given over to an order of 'penitent women', though it is also possible there was a convent on the site in earlier centuries. The Order of Preachers (the Dominicans) took it over probably in the 1260s: their main house was at **Santa Sabina**, on the Aventine, so they needed a centrally located church and house. The building of the church began about 1280, when Gothic architecture was at its height, and it remains the only medieval Gothic church in Rome, though there are several neo-Gothic ones from the nineteenth century. It is, however, so overlaid with Renaissance additions (including the façade) that its 'Gothic-ness' is not easy to see. Construction took many years, not least because of the exile in Avignon of the papacy throughout much of the fourteenth century, swiftly followed by the Great Western Schism which lasted until the second decade of the fifteenth. Over this century and more many of Rome's great buildings became derelict, not least the papal cathedral, St John Lateran, and as a consequence Santa Maria sopra Minerva was chosen as the setting for the election of Pope Eugenius IV in 1431 and his successor Nicholas V in 1447.

The church contains a remarkable collection of monuments. On the right-hand transept is the Carafa chapel, donated by Cardinal Oliviero Carafa (1430–1511) who in 1472 was the admiral of the papal fleet in a largely successful expedition against the Turks. The chapel is dedicated to the Dominican theologian Thomas Aquinas who was claimed by Oliviero's mother as a distant relative. One of the frescoes – they are by Filippino Lippi – shows St Thomas overcoming heresy. Two small boys in the fresco are future popes, both Medicis, Leo X (1513–21) and Clement VII (1523–34), whose monuments are situated behind the high altar. It was Leo X whose promotion of the sale of indulgences to finance the building of St Peter's so angered Martin Luther, and Clement VII was the pope who refused Henry VIII of England his divorce. The Carafa

*The shrine, in the Dominican church of Santa Maria sopra Minerva, is of the saint and mystic Catherine of Siena (1347–80) who in 1970 was declared a Doctor of the Church.*

chapel houses the tomb of Pope Paul IV, Giampietro Carafa, a nephew of Oliviero in whose household he grew up, who served as Leo X's legate to the court of Henry VIII. He was unremittingly hostile to Protestantism, revived the Inquisition, created the Index of forbidden books, and confined Roman Jews to a ghetto.

On the left side of the high altar is a sculpture by Michelangelo of Christ carrying his cross. Beneath the high altar is the tomb of St Catherine of Siena (Caterina Benincasa, 1347–80), a mystic and a Dominican nun. In 1376 she visited Pope Gregory XI in Avignon and bolstered his resolve to return the papacy to Rome. In 1378 she went to Rome to encourage Urban VI in his efforts to reform the Church, efforts which alienated many of the cardinals and led directly to the Great Western Schism. Catherine died in Rome, was canonized in 1461, declared patron saint of Italy in 1939 and named a Doctor of the Church in 1970, the first woman to be elevated to that status. The room in which she died was close by in a house in the Via di S Chiara. Her body was moved to a chapel to the right of the high altar, and this remained her shrine from 1451 to 1855 when her remains (apart from her head, which was returned to Siena in 1381) were installed in their current position before the high altar. To the left of the choir is a passageway leading out of the church at the rear. There is a memorial in the passage to mark the burial place of the Dominican John of Fiesole, better known as Fra Angelico (c. 1395–1455), who was beatified in 1982 and declared patron saint of artists. He is best known for his work at the Dominican house of San Marco in Florence, but for the last decade of his life he was in Rome, working on the chapel of Pope Nicholas V in the Vatican. He died at Santa Maria sopra Minerva. On the left-hand side of the church is the chapel dedicated to Pope St Pius V (1566–72), a Dominican. Below the altar of the chapel is a glass box containing the relics of a martyr, St Vittoria, of whom nothing is known except that, from the wax effigy, she must have been a child. It was in this church, which for a time served as the headquarters of the Inquisition, that Galileo was forced, in 1633, to deny that the sun was stable and the earth went round it. *Via del Beato Angelico 35 / Piazza della Minerva 42*


## San Martino ai Monti (St Martin on the Hills)

This minor basilica is dedicated to St Martin of Tours (c. 316–97), a soldier who became a 'conscientious objector' to military service after converting to Christianity. He was imprisoned but later released and became the bishop of Tours and the founder of monasticism in what is now France. It is likely, however, that this was not the original dedication. It was founded on the site of a house owned by a priest called Equitius by Pope St Sylvester I (314–35), and may have been dedicated to him: the modern official dedication is to both Sylvester and Martin, which is that of Pope Symmachus (498–514) when he had it rebuilt. It may have been that there were two churches very close together, one dedicated to Sylvester and the other to Martin. The story of it being built on a priest's residence is unlikely. There are earlier Roman buildings beneath and to one side, but they more resemble a shopping arcade than a house.

The present building is of the ninth century, built in 845 by Pope Sergius II (844–47), though several times restored – the decoration of the interior is largely from the seventeenth century. It is claimed that the relics of Pope Sergius are enshrined here, although he was first buried in old St Peter's. Sergius is said to have brought to Rome and interred in this church the relics of Pope St Martin I (649–55) who died in the Crimea, having been driven into exile by the Emperor allegedly for supporting a rebel exarch – the one who had been sent to arrest him – but in reality for opposing the Emperor's religious policy. Because of the brutality with which he was treated, and his death in prison, he has been regarded as a martyr. There are numerous other relics of Roman martyrs in the church, brought there in the ninth century because of the threat to the outlying catacombs from invaders. The church has been in the charge of the Calced (shoe-wearing) Carmelites since the end of the thirteenth century. They ran what now would be called a homeless shelter where St Benedict Joseph Labre would stay when the weather was too unpleasant for him to sleep in the arches of the Colosseum. This has been a titular church since the end of the thirteenth century, and one of the cardinals whose title it became was William Allen (1532–94), the exiled Lancashire-born leader of English Catholics in the latter half of the sixteenth century. *Viale Monte Oppio 28*

# Santi Nereo e Achilleo (SS Nereus and Achilleus)

The dedication of this minor basilica is to two soldier saints who were martyred in the fourth century and were originally buried in the catacomb of St Domitilla. It is a very old church, first mentioned with the name 'Titulus Fasciolae' in the late fourth century. The origin of the name is disputed, partly because the meaning of the Latin word 'fasciolae' is uncertain. It could mean 'bandage', with the suggestion that it was on the site of this church that St Peter, as related in some apocryphal acts, took off the bandage he had tied around his leg after it had been held in irons. The dedication of the church to Nereus and Achilleus took place sometime before the end of the sixth century. It is reasonable to assume that the saints' relics were moved from the catacomb at this time and enshrined in the church, though it is not clear why.

It is, however, much more likely that the relics came to the church in 814 when it was rebuilt, though on a slightly different site, in the pontificate of Leo III (795–816): it is Pope Leo's church that survives beneath the baroque embellishments of the great Oratorian ecclesiastical historian Cardinal Caesar Baronius (1538–1607), who was for a time the titular priest. The church was at this time given over to the Oratorians, who still serve here. As a historian, Baronius was eager to preserve as much as possible of the early medieval church and the restoration was well done. A bishop's chair stands in the apse, apparently reconstructed by Baronius, who had inscribed on it Pope Gregory the Great's (590–604) sermon which the Pope said he was delivering before the shrine of Nereus and Achilleus. It is, however, now presumed that this was delivered not in the church but in the catacomb of St Domitilla, in which case the two martyrs' relics would not yet have been transferred. They are now enshrined beneath the high altar, though their heads were taken at the end of the sixteenth century to the Oratorians' **Chiesa Nuova**. Also beneath the high altar are the relics of St Domitilla, who is a rather more mysterious character. Legend, and it is little more than that, has it that she was the niece, or possibly the wife, of the consul Titus Flavius Clemens. He was put to death in the first century for atheism, which might possibly mean that he converted to Christianity. Domitilla, however, was at first exiled to an island (Ponza) and either died or was put to death there, her relics later being brought to Rome to the catacomb which bears her name. *Via delle Terme di Caracalla 28*

## San Nicola da Tolentino agli Orti Sallustiani
(St Nicholas of Tolentino at the Gardens of Sallust)

Nicholas of Tolentino (1235–1305) was an Augustinian friar renowned as a wonder-worker especially in Tolentino in the Marche region of Italy where he spent the last years of his life. This church was founded by Augustinians in the last years of the sixteenth century. As a place of pilgrimage it is of little general interest. However, it is the national church in Rome of those Armenians who are in communion with the papacy, and their college is next door to the church. The Armenians also have a more centrally located church, San Biagio della Pagnotta. *Salita S Nicola da Tolentino 17*

## San Nicola in Carcere (St Nicholas in Prison)

The name is a puzzle. The church is dedicated to the fourth-century St Nicholas, bishop of Myra (Mugla in modern Turkey) – 'Santa Claus' – but there is no evidence that there was ever a prison on this site, though part of the Nicholas legend has him in prison for a time. His was a very popular cult in the East and, especially after his relics had been brought to Bari in Italy in 1087, in the West as well. It has been proposed that this church was dedicated to him because it was located in a part of Rome with a heavily Greek population. The origins of the church are obscure, and its existence is certain only from the eleventh century. It was several times restored, wholly rebuilt at the end of the sixteenth century and renovated several times since. It is particularly interesting archaeologically with the temple of Janus on one side of it, that of Spes (Hope) on the other and of Juno beneath it. Moreover its campanile was once a fortified tower of the powerful Pierleoni family, converts to Christianity from Judaism, who played an important part in the history of the church in the twelfth century – one member, Pietro Pierleoni, became Pope Anacletus II (1130–38). He is usually listed as an antipope, but his election was no more irregular than that of his 'opponent', Innocent II (1130–43). The stronghold of the Pierleoni family was beside San Nicola, and in the thirteenth century it appears to have borne their name.

As a place of pilgrimage, the relics under the main altar are those of Mark and Marcellian, twin brothers who were martyred in 280, as well as Simplician, Faustinus and Viatrix, two brothers and their sister (Viatrix is also identified as Beatrice), who were martyred on the road outside Rome in 304. Rather more significant, perhaps, than the saints are two chapels, dedicated respectively to Our Lady of Pompeii, a late-nineteenth-century devotion which has a large following in Italy in general, and to Our Lady of Guadalupe, which makes the church a centre of devotion for Latin Americans, especially Mexicans, living in Rome. *Via del Teatro di Marcello 46 / Via del Foro Olitorio*

## Santissimo Nome di Maria al Foro Traiano
(The Most Holy Name of Mary at the
Forum of Trajan)

In July 1683 the army of the Ottoman Turks arrived at
the outskirts of Vienna – and not for the first time. But
the 1683 siege proved to be the apogee of Ottoman power
in Europe. The city was relieved by an army led by Jan
Sobieski III, King of Poland, on 12 September. To mark
the victory Pope Innocent XI (1676–89) instituted the feast
of the Most Holy Name of Mary, and not long afterwards
a confraternity was founded to propagate devotion to the
feast. It was established in the church of St Bernard at the
Column of Trajan, but this proved too small for the number of devotees and another church, the present SS Nome
de Maria, was built next to it between 1736 and 1741,
the old St Bernard's being pulled down soon afterwards.
There had, however, been in the old church an icon of the
Madonna claimed to have been painted by St Luke. This
icon, to which there was, and is, a considerable devotion,
was moved from St Bernard's and is now prominently displayed above the main altar. *Foro Traiano 89*

## San Pancrazio (St Pancras)

There used to be much amusement among small Catholic
boys and girls reading their English missals when they came
across the rubric 'Station at St Pancras'. There is, however, a
slim connection between the stational church of St Pancras
in Rome and the London railway station from which trains
depart for the continent. The station takes its name from
the nearby Old St Pancras Church which occupies a site,
so it is claimed, of Christian worship from the fourth century. The dedication to St Pancras originated, it seems,

with monks who came to England in the eleventh century, and who were under the impression that Benedictines had served the Roman St Pancras in the early Middle Ages. St Pancras himself seems to have been a fourteen-year-old youth who was martyred in the persecution of Diocletian. His tomb became a catacomb, and a small church was built on the site. This in turn was rebuilt as a pilgrimage church by Pope Honorius I (625–38), and it is this church, though much restored down the centuries, which survives today. Honorius placed the relics of the young martyr in the crypt. These, however, were dispersed by the French during their occupation of the city at the end of the eighteenth century, and all that remains now, in a reliquary in the right-hand aisle, is a small fragment of the saint's head which had been in the Lateran basilica. The church is located within the park of the Villa Doria Pamphilj, and is not easily reached: though once one of Rome's most important pilgrimage churches it now receives few visitors. It is served by the Discalced Carmelites. *Piazza San Pancrazio 5D*

## San Pantaleo (St Pantaleon)

The saint to whom this church is dedicated is much venerated in the East, less so in the West, though some towns in France, for instance, bear versions of his name. The tradition is that he was a doctor who converted back to Christianity after lapsing, gave away his considerable fortune and was martyred in 303, becoming the patron saint, or one of them, of the medical profession. The origins of the church are not known, though it was in existence by the late twelfth century. In 1611 it was handed over to a new religious order, founded by the Spanish-born St Joseph Calasanz or Calasanctius (1557–1648), and a school was created for twelve hundred pupils. It went on to become the mother-house of the Poor Clerks Regular of the Mother of God of the Pious Schools, better known as the Piarists or Scolopi (the latter name comes from the Italian 'scuole pie' or pious schools). The saint, who suffered the indignity of being suspended from his own religious order and seeing the order suppressed (it survived as a society of diocesan clergy and was only restored in 1656) through the machinations of one of its members, is interred beneath the high altar. After the order was restored the church was largely rebuilt, but St Joseph's room in the neighbouring house was kept exactly as it was in his lifetime and can be visited. *Piazza San Pantaleo / Piazza dei Massimi 4*

## San Paolo alla Regola
(St Paul in the schoolroom – but see below)

Although this is a seventeenth-century building, there is documentary evidence of a church on this site from the very end of the twelfth century. Tradition claims it is much older, dating from the second century, and that it was erected on the spot where St Paul taught the faith while awaiting trial. The room where this is supposed to have happened is preserved, and the name could be taken to mean 'St Paul at his schoolroom', though this interpretation is challenged. The area was, however, a place where tanners worked, to whom Paul, as a tent-maker, would have related. For the same reason, Paul would have been a natural patron saint for the tanners' guild, which may be why there is this dedication to him. However, Luff points out that an early life of Paul says that while in Rome he hired a granary in which to do his teaching, and excavations have found traces of a granary nearby. *Via di San Paolo alla Regola 6*

*This fourteenth-century icon, known as Our Lady of Graces, showing the Madonna breastfeeding her son, is to be found in the church of San Paolo alla Regola, a name which perhaps translates as 'St Paul at the Place of Teaching'.*

## San Paolo alle Tre Fontane
(St Paul at the Three Fountains)

For the story of the three fountains, see **San Paolo fuori le Mura**. The origins of this pilgrimage church date at least to the early seventh century, and may be older. The three fountains, or springs, used to flow into this church, rebuilt at the very end of the sixteenth century, but have apparently dried up. In the right-hand corner of the nave is a column, claimed to be the one to which St Paul was tied before his execution. *Via Acque Salvie 1*

## San Pietro in Montorio (St Peter's on Golden Hill)

The name 'golden hill' dates from medieval times, but its origin is unclear. It was then believed that this was the site of the martyrdom of the Apostle Peter – it is now as certain as it can be (there is no absolute proof that Peter was ever in Rome) that he died in the Circus of Nero. There is a fairly simple explanation for the mistake. The *Acts of Peter* – which themselves cannot be trusted even though they were composed very early – say he was executed between two 'metae'. The 'meta' was the turning point in races. That obviously would fit with the Circus, but the word can also mean 'pyramid', and the medieval scholars thought they had identified the two pyramids, placing this church between them.

There was a monastery here from at least the early ninth century, and the church was rebuilt in the last decades of the fifteenth century after Franciscans had taken it over: they are still in charge. It was here that St Ignatius Loyola came to pray for guidance before accepting the office of Superior General of the Society of Jesus. Buried in the crypt are Earl Hugh O'Neill of Tyrone (1540–1616) and

Rory O'Donnell (1575–1608), the first Earl of Tyrconnell, together with some of their followers in 'the flight of the earls' from Ulster in 1607. The church has a particularly impressive interior but no shrines of interest to pilgrims (other, perhaps, than to the Irish). Beside it is the rather beautiful 'Tempietto', a separate little chapel built by Bramante in the first decade of the sixteenth century. This was believed – though no longer – to be the exact location of Peter's martyrdom. Ignatius used to come here to say mass. This shrine on the Janiculum is no longer much visited, which is a pity. *Piazza San Pietro in Montorio 2*

## *San Pietro in Vincoli (St Peter in Chains)

In the second century BC there were houses on this site belonging to wealthy families. In the first century AD they were replaced, apparently, by part of a palace. In the third century a large hall was built here, possibly for Christian worship though there is no direct evidence of that. Sometime, and it is not known when, a church was definitely constructed and dedicated to the twelve apostles. The priest Philip, who attended the Council of Ephesus in 431, was in charge of this church and a few years after the Council, along with someone called Eudoxia, decided to construct the new basilica, changing the dedication to SS Peter and Paul. The name was formally changed to the present one during the pontificate of Pope St Gregory VII (1073–85) though apparently it had informally been known as Peter in Chains for centuries. The church gained that title because it possessed the chains which bound St Peter. When they arrived is not clear, but the story attributes one of them to a gift of Eudoxia, who brought it back from Jerusalem. The other chain is said to be that which bound him when he was in Rome. In the middle of the fifth century the two miraculously fused together, and they can now be seen in a reliquary in the 'confessio' in front of the main altar. These chains proved an enormous attraction to medieval pilgrims, and the fame of the church spread far beyond Rome: the chapel in the Tower of London, to take one instance, is dedicated to St Peter in Chains. While one is entirely entitled to treat the story with considerable scepticism, the basilica was built close by the headquarters of the Urban Prefect, or city governor, and the complex included a prison of the type in which Peter, had he been incarcerated in Rome as is generally believed, would have been held.

The basilica, which has long been administered by the Canons Regular of the Lateran, is still basically a fifth-century construction, though it has been much restored, and it contains a mosaic representing St Sebastian who was martyred in the early fourth century, according to tradition, by being beaten to death with clubs after he had survived being shot by arrows. It shows him as a bearded, elderly man, quite unlike later depictions which tend to show him as a beardless youth. It was erected in 680. In the crypt there is a fourth-century Christian sarcophagus put there by Pope Pelagius (556–61) to hold the relics of the (Jewish) Maccabean martyrs, the seven brothers who were put to death for refusing to break the Law of Moses. Unfortunately when the sarcophagus was opened it was found to contain animal bones, and the crypt is now kept locked.

Many of the visitors who flock to the church, however, come not to see the chains but Michelangelo's statue of Moses: so many come that a one-way system has had to be introduced for those wishing to view it. This statue, famously depicted with horns because of a mistranslation of the Hebrew (Moses came down the mountain not with horns on his head by rays of light!), is part of a monu-

*The chains which reputedly bound St Peter can be venerated in the 'confessio' beneath the high altar of San Pietro in Vincoli (St Peter in Chains). The reliquary itself dates from the mid-nineteenth century.*

mental funerary sculpture commissioned for his own tomb by Pope Julius II (1502–13) but never finished. Parts of the sculpture can be found in museums elsewhere (not in Rome), but the Moses is the most substantial section, indeed far too big for the location in which it is now found. It was placed in the church in 1545, though Pope Julius was in the end buried in St Peter's in the Vatican: St Peter in Chains had been his titular church when he was a cardinal. *Piazza San Pietro in Vincoli 4A*

## *Santa Prassede (St Praxedes)

The person to whom this minor basilica is dedicated is almost certainly not formally a saint, and has been dropped from the Roman Martyrology. Unlike her putative sister St Pudentiana (see the entry for **Santa Pudenziana**), however, she may well have been a donor to an earlier version of this particularly interesting church which, because of its proximity to Santa Maria Maggiore, is often overlooked. The 'titulus' of St Praxedes certainly existed by the end of the fifth century, but the present church was built by Pope St Paschal I (817–24), very possibly not on the same site as the earlier one: the first Santa Prassede had been constructed, like Santa Pudenziana, on the foundations of a Roman bath house. It was Pope Paschal who commissioned the array of mosaics which is one of the glories of the church, if not indeed of Rome itself, and ought not to be missed.

There was a monastery attached to the church, which was first staffed by Greek-rite monks, in Rome quite possibly as refugees from iconoclasm, but later, and until the present day, by Benedictine monks of the Vallumbrosan Congregation. St Charles Borromeo (1538–94), the great reforming archbishop of Milan whose titular church this was, used to stay in the monastery when he was in Rome, and the table from which he fed the poor of the area is still to be found in the church. In the 'confessio' are two sarcophagi, supposedly containing the relics of SS Pudentiana and Praxedes which were found in a small room during one of the restorations, together with the sarcophagi: one of Pope Paschal's reasons for his church-building was to house relics which, because of marauders around Rome, had to be brought into the city from the early Christian cemeteries. Near the entrance to the church is a thirteenth-century icon, the Madonna della Salute, Our Lady of Health,

*This broken column, in the church of Santa Prassede, arrived in Rome from the Holy Land in the early thirteenth century and is venerated as that to which Christ was tied during the scourging.*

which is the object of much devotion. The mosaics on the triumphal arch and in the apse date from the pontificate of Paschal: the one in the apse shows Christ standing in clouds flanked by the apostles Peter and Paul. The apostles have their arms around the two sisters Pudentiana and Praxedes, who are dressed like Byzantine princesses. Pope Paschal is himself represented, holding a model of the church – people claim to see a family likeness with the representation of his mother Theodora (see below). At the bottom of the nave is a large porphyry roundel which, according to tradition, marks the well down which Praxedes poured the blood of the martyrs she had soaked up with her sponge: the sponge is said to be with her remains in the 'confessio'.

The chapel of the cross contains a crucifix before which prayed St Bridget of Sweden (1303–73) who, after giving birth to eight children, and after the death of her husband, came to Rome to seek approval for the order she had founded, the Brigettines. The crucifix is said to have spoken to her. It is, however, unclear whether the crucifix in the chapel is the same one. The chapel of St Zeno, with its impressive ninth-century mosaics, was intended by Pope Paschal as a mausoleum for his mother, Theodora: there is a dedication, 'Theodora episcopa', which has suggested to some that there were women bishops in the medieval Church. Little or nothing is known of Zeno, said to be a Roman martyr: his relics are enshrined in the chapel. Next to the chapel of St Zeno is that of the Pillar of Scourging, the pillar to which Christ was tied, in other words, during his Passion. It was brought from the Holy Land in 1223: there is, however, another and rather more likely pillar still in Jerusalem's Church of the Holy Sepulchre. Its presence here accounts for the many frescoes depicting the Passion. The chapel of St Pius X (1903–14) has several relics displayed in glass cases. At the end of the left aisle and set into the wall is a black marble slab, claimed to be the bed of St Praxedes. In the sacristy are preserved relics of Christ, a piece of the seamless garment removed from him at the crucifixion, and a small piece of the crown of thorns. *Via de Santa Prassede 9A / Via San Martino ai Monti*

## *Santa Prisca (St Prisca)

There have been efforts made to identify this saint with the Priscilla named in the New Testament, and indeed to claim that Peter and Paul both stayed in her house on this spot. None of this is very convincing. When excavations were undertaken it was discovered that the church was constructed over a Mithraeum, rather like **San Clemente**. To get to the Mithraeum one has to pass through the crypt, where the relics claimed to be those of St Prisca are in the altar. Of more interest is the baptistery, on the left as one enters. The font is made out of an ancient column with its capital, the basin itself being the hollowed-out capital. It is claimed that this font was used by St Peter, though the saint, had he ever conducted baptisms in Rome, would have done so by some form of immersion, not in a font of this shape. *Via di Santa Prisca 11*

## *Santa Pudenziana (St Pudentiana)

There never was, as far as is known, any saint called Pudentiana. Pudentiana is quite probably an adjectival form of the name Pudens, and the original name (title) of the church was 'titulus' Pudentis: the 'Pudenziana' stems only from the eighth century. The legend, which is important to the history of this minor basilica, is that this was the house of Pudens, with whom St Peter stayed when he came to Rome, and that Pudens had two daughters, Pudentiana and Praxedes, both of whom were claimed as virgin martyrs: they are depicted in the frieze in the vestibule of the church carrying vessels in which to collect the blood of the martyrs. Unfortunately the story is false: although the building does indeed date back to the very early Christian era in Rome, it was unquestionably a bath house, and the bath house was adapted into a church at the end of the fourth century, and completed in the early fifth century. The mosaic in the apse is one of the finest, and almost certainly the oldest, Christian mosaic in Rome. It depicts Christ with the Apostles, and two female figures who might be SS Pudentiana and Praxedes, but these figures are more likely to represent the church of the synagogue and the church of the gentiles, a witness to the effort to bring together the 'gentile' and the 'Jewish' Christian communities in Rome at that period. In the background there are a number of buildings which may be intended to represent the churches erected by Constantine in the Holy Land. The chapel of St Pudens contains part of a wooden altar: it is claimed that St Peter celebrated the Eucharist on this table while staying in the house of Pudens. This basilica is the national church in Rome for Filipinos. *Via Urbana 160*

## Santi Quattro Coronati
## (The Church of the Four Crowned Martyrs)

*The remarkable series of paintings, executed in 1246, in the chapel of St Sylvester attached to the church of the Santi Quattro Coronati (The Four Holy Crowned Ones) depicts the mythical life of Pope St Sylvester (314–35), in which the Emperor Constantine is cured of leprosy by the Pope, and is baptized by him. This picture shows Constantine, his face spotted by leprosy, dreaming of SS Peter and Paul.*

Visitors accustomed to the late antique or baroque style of Roman churches will be surprised by this fortress-like building halfway between San Clemente and the Lateran. It was fortified in this style by Pope Innocent IV (1243–54) soon after his election precisely as a place of refuge: he felt himself too vulnerable at the Lateran in the long conflict between papacy and empire which dominated much of the thirteenth century. There had been an earlier church on this site, but the date of its foundation remains unclear; it may have been erected in the late fourth century, or possibly slightly later. This was restored several times until it was destroyed by the Normans in 1084, then rebuilt by Pope Paschal II (1099–1118) and consecrated in 1116.

The other mystery is – or are – the four saints, not least because there seem to have been rather more than four. The relics of five martyred Persian stonemasons were brought to the church by Pope Leo IV (847–55). An alternative version is that the martyrs were four Roman soldiers, martyred for refusing to offer sacrifice to a pagan god, who were buried by Pope Miltiades (311–14) on the Via Labicana which runs by the present church. The Four Crowned Martyrs, whoever they were, at one time enjoyed a considerable cult: their relics are contained in sarcophagi in the crypt. The head of St Sebastian, the Roman soldier who according to a much later legend was shot to death by arrows at the end of the third century, is kept at an altar on the left-hand side of the church. Also on the left of the nave is the entrance to the cloisters, and off the (very attractive) cloister is the chapel of St Barbara which appears to date from the first church on the site and is the guild chapel of stonemasons. This minor basilica is served, as it has been from the middle of the sixteenth century, by Augustinian priests. However, if you wish to visit the cloister and – especially – the remarkable series of frescoes in the chapel of St Sylvester you will have to be admitted by nuns from the convent beside the church. The frescoes tell the (entirely apocryphal) story of the conversion of Constantine and his baptism by Pope Sylvester I (314–35). *Piazza dei Santi Quattro Coronati 20*

## San Rocco (St Rocco, Roche or Roque)

The saint to whom this church is dedicated is little known in England but his cult is widespread in Europe. His dates are uncertain, but he lived in the second half of the four-teenth century, dying c. 1380. He is usually depicted as a pilgrim, which he was, and accompanied by a little dog, often with bread in its mouth. The story is that he caught the plague (the Black Death was endemic in Europe at the time) and retired to a forest to die, but was fed by a dog which brought him food: in images there is a mark of the plague on his leg. Against all odds he recovered, and sub-sequently gained a reputation for healing. This church was originally the chapel of a hospital, built in the late fifteenth century by Tiber boatmen. It went on to develop a wing for pregnant women who were allowed, should they so wish, to remain anonymous. A church dedicated to St Martin of Tours was demolished to make way for the new building, and a chapel dedicated to St Martin is still to be found in the church. Its period of expansion, however, was in the 1650s after an image of Our Lady of Graces, a copy of one in the church of Santa Maria delle Grazie al Foro Romano, came to be regarded as miraculous, and the centre of devo-tion to the Virgin. In the sacristy is a reliquary containing a hand of St Rocco. The hospital itself was closed at the beginning of the twentieth century. *Largo San Rocco 1*

## San Saba (St Sabas)

St Sabas (439–532) was born in Cappadocia but spent most of his life in Palestine where he lived a quasi-eremitical existence even though he founded a famous, and still extant, monastery. The foundation myth for this church claims that it was an oratory built by St Sylvia, the mother of Pope St Gregory I, on the site of her house. Excavations have revealed, however, that it was a mid-seventh-century foundation, clearly built for Eastern monks, those who had fled Palestine after it had been overrun by Persians. For a couple of centuries it was a very important monastery of Greek monks, but then passed through several monastic communities before being given, in the 1930s, into the care of the Society of Jesus. (It had for a time belonged to the Germano-Hungarian College, which was run by Jesuits.) Though much restored over the centuries, what is to be seen is basically a tenth- and eleventh-century church. There is a relic of St Sabas under the main altar: his chief relics had been in Venice but were restored to the monastery of St Sabas in Palestine by Pope Paul VI. On one wall is a fresco illustrating the life of St Nicholas of Myra ('Santa Claus'), which shows three naked young ladies in bed, with Nicholas looking in. According to his life, he knew that the family was extremely poor, and to save the girls from a life of prostitution he secretly gave them gold coins – which the fresco depicts him about to do. *Piazza Bernini 20*

## *Santa Sabina (St Sabina)

Some guides to Rome list this church on the Aventine as that which perhaps most accurately recalls the early Christian basilicas. Its interior has occasionally been remodelled, thus destroying the general impression of an early basilica, but the exterior is much as it was when it was first constructed in the early fifth century, possibly c. 425. There is a grating in the floor allowing sight of a Roman house which may have been the original 'titulus', possibly belonging to someone called Sabina, for although the relics of a St Sabina (and three otherwise unknown martyrs, Alexander, Theodolus and Eventius) are enshrined beneath the high altar, the tradition concerning a saint called Sabina is entirely legendary. Since 1218 Santa Sabina has been in the care of Dominican friars, and it serves as their Rome headquarters. This means that many important members of the Order lived here, including SS Dominic (c. 1170–1221), Thomas Aquinas (c. 1225–74), Hyacinth (1185–1257) and Pope Pius V (1504–72), Pope Pius being the one who in 1570 excommunicated Queen Elizabeth I of England. It is possible to visit the friary and see the rooms used by Dominic and Pope Pius (before he became pope, of course), and to see an orange tree just outside the basilica which is said to be descended from one planted by Dominic himself. The main doors, of cypress wood, are particularly interesting, for they are made up of painted panels – though some are missing – which appear to be contemporary with the church's original construction in the fifth century. *Piazza Pietro d'Illiria 1*

## San Salvatore in Lauro
([Church of] the Holy Saviour by the Laurel Tree)

Apparently a twelfth-century foundation but entirely rebuilt c. 1450, then again after a disastrous fire in 1591, this church has one of the most beautiful of Roman cloisters, constructed for the Augustinian canons who for a while inhabited the neighbouring convent. Beyond the cloister there is a small garden. In the refectory of the convent there is the tomb of Pope Eugenius IV (1431–47) which was moved there when St Peter's was being rebuilt in the sixteenth century. *Piazza San Salvatore in Lauro 15*

## San Salvatore in Onda
([Church of] the Holy Saviour on the Wave)

The name is a bit odd. 'Onda' means wave, as in the sea, but it can also mean a surge or a flood, and probably refers to the River Tiber bursting its banks which it used to do fairly often. This church was first built in the eleventh century, entirely rebuilt in the thirteenth, and there were major restorations in the late seventeenth and late nineteenth centuries, so that only the crypt remains as a visible reminder of the medieval building, though seemingly much of the original structure exists beneath the various restorations. The church is not of great interest in itself, but in a glass case under the high altar, and partially observable, lies the incorrupt body of St Vincent Pallotti (1795–1850), founder of the Society of the Catholic Apostolate (the Pallottine Fathers who run the church), who engage particularly in work among the poor. His rooms, now a museum, may be visited. In front of the altar of the chapel dedicated to Our Lady as Virgo Potens – Powerful Virgin – is buried Elizabeth Sanna (1788–1857), the widowed mother of seven children. She came to Rome while on her way to the Holy Land, and stayed, associating herself with the Pallottines in their work among the poor and the sick. She donated the icon in this chapel, and was declared Venerable in 2014. *Via dei Pettinari 51*

# San Sebastiano fuori le Mura
## (St Sebastian Outside the Walls)

*This sculpture of the dying St Sebastian is by Giuseppe
Giorgetti, who flourished in the second half of the
seventeenth century – his exact dates are uncertain. It
is to be found in the basilica of San Sebastiano fuori le
Mura (St Sebastian Outside the Walls).*

The dedication of this basilica, originally a fourth-century
construction, was first to the Apostles Peter and Paul whose
bodies were thought to have been moved to this spot during
a mid-third-century persecution. There are still graffiti
extant which witness to this. However, in the ninth century
the dedication was changed to St Sebastian, the late-third-
century martyr who, according to tradition, had been tied
to a pillar and used as target practice by archers. His tomb
is to be found in this basilica, marked by a statue of the
dying saint, together with the pillar and one of the arrows.
These are kept in the chapel of the relics, where there is also
a stone slab marked, apparently, with a footprint. This is
said to be a footprint left by Christ when he met Peter as
the Apostle fled Rome, and met Christ going the other way.
'*Domine, quo vadis?*', 'Master, where are you going?' Peter

is said to have asked, and when Christ responded that he was going to Rome to be crucified, Peter turned back into the city to meet his death. There is a church, or pilgrimage shrine, at the spot where Christ appeared, though the earliest references to it are only from the ninth century. Also in San Sebastiano are the tombs of St Quirinus, martyred in what is now Croatia in 309 but whose relics were brought to Rome in the fifth century, and the martyr Pope St Fabian (236–50). It is possible here to visit the catacombs of St Sebastian. It may well have been this basilica which in a sense coined the name 'catacomb' from the Greek meaning 'near the hollow' – possibly a valley or quarry – which was the name of the spot in ancient times. There were pagan burials here, and then Christian ones, and the basilica was built over them. These catacombs, unlike others in Rome, were never forgotten, and the name 'near the hollow' came to be applied to all similar burial sites. The basilica is now in the charge of the Friars Minor. *Via Appia Antica 136*

## San Silvestro al Quirinale
(St Sylvester's by the Quirinal)

The Quirinal, or often Quirinale, is the official residence of the presidents – and before that of the kings – of Italy, but it was built in 1583 as a summer residence for the papacy, standing as it does on the highest of Rome's seven hills. As a papal residence it housed four nineteenth-century conclaves, and the cardinals processed into the palace from the nearby church of St Sylvester. The Sylvester of the dedication is Pope St Sylvester (314–35) and the story of his relationship with Constantine, entirely legendary though it be, is represented in the iconography. In a chapel on the right-hand side there is a much revered thirteenth-century icon called the Madonna della Catena, 'Our Lady of the

*This rather curious picture shows a thirteenth-century Madonna, Our Lady of the Chain, within a sixteenth-century one which shows the icon being venerated by Pope St Pius V (1566–72) and Cardinal Antonio Carafa (1538–91).*

Chain': it is located within a sixteenth-century painting. This apart, there are no significant relics here. But the church is nonetheless of considerable interest to English and Welsh pilgrims because it is the burial place of Thomas Goldwell (d. 1585), bishop of St Asaph in North Wales, and the only English bishop to have attended the Council of Trent – though only the last (1563) session. He was a member of the Theatine Order which looked after the church, and he was himself for a time the superior of the community there. The year before his death he consecrated the high altar in the church, which is now looked after by the Missionaries of St Vincent de Paul, commonly known as Lazarists. *Via Ventiquattro (XXIV) Maggio*


## San Silvestro in Capite
(St Sylvester's – the 'in Capite' is explained below)

When relics of the martyrs had to be 'repatriated' from the catacombs because of marauding bands in the latter part of the eighth century, the church of St Sylvester was built to receive them: those which came are listed at the entrance to the church, the most significant being those of St Tarcisius who was martyred in Rome as he was carrying the consecrated hosts – possibly intended for imprisoned Christians, but perhaps from one church to another as was the practice. Legend has him as a young boy, but that is not certain: indeed, his whole existence is uncertain because he is not included in the earliest lists of martyrs. His relics, and those of other martyrs, including Pope St Stephen I (254–57) and Pope St Dionysus (260–68), were interred beneath the altar, and there is a modern (1906) 'confessio' leading down towards them.

The most significant relic in this church, however, is the head ('in Capite') of John the Baptist which is in a chapel to the left of the entrance. There is certainly a head contained in the reliquary, but unfortunately more than one church claims to have this particular relic. It has been venerated in Rome since the middle of the twelfth century when it was in a nearby church: it has been here since the thirteenth century, when the church was in the care of the Poor Clares. It may have been brought to Rome by the Greek-rite monks who were in charge of the church at its foundation: they were probably refugees from iconoclasm. John the Baptist is portrayed in the iconography, but so is the figure of Christ – or his face. This is because the church at one time housed the 'Mandylion', a portrait of the head of Christ on cloth. According to legend Christ imprinted his face on the cloth and sent it to Abgar, the King of Edessa. This miraculous image was recorded as being in Edessa in the middle of the sixth century, but was transferred to Constantinople in the tenth and was in San Silvestro by the early sixteenth century, but is now – since 1870 – kept in a chapel in the Vatican Palace. The church, which stands back from the road, was rebuilt in the late sixteenth century, and now is in the charge of the Pallottine Fathers. It is the national church for Great Britain, and in general serves the English-speaking population of Rome. *Piazza San Silvestro*

## *San Sisto Vecchio (The Old St Sixtus)

Sixtus II – or, more correctly, Xystus II – was Bishop of Rome for only a year, from August 257 to August 258. He was beheaded in the Cemetery of Praetextatus: the bloodstained episcopal chair in which he had been sitting was placed in the chapel of the Cemetery (Catacomb) of Callistus where he was buried: seven of his deacons were executed on the same day. Pope Paschal I (817–24) brought his body into St Peter's, but Leo IV (847–55) moved his relics to San Sisto where they remain. This minor basilica dates from the fourth or early fifth century – it may have been one of the 'tituli' though this is uncertain – and had to be substantially remodelled in the first decades of the thirteenth century: this is the building which survives today, at least in its exterior appearance. After its remodelling it was handed over to St Dominic, who lived here for a time before moving to **Santa Sabina**. *Piazzale Numa Pompilio 8*


## Santo Spirito in Sassia
(The Church of the Holy Spirit)

As one guidebook remarks, there is nothing of interest in this church. It has been included because the 'in Sassia' (the original name was Santa Maria in Sassia, and was changed in the early thirteenth century) means 'among the Saxons': the Saxons, in this instance, being the English who had settled in what is now the Borgo, which itself comes from the same root as 'borough'. There is a set of frescoes which depicts the history of the 'schola Saxonum', the hospice for English pilgrims, the remote ancestor of the Venerable English College. The building itself is from the sixteenth century. *Via dei Penitenzieri 12*


## *Santo Stefano Rotondo al Celio
(St Stephen's Round Church on the Coelian Hill)

This church, which is rather hidden away and has to be approached through a gateway which is easy to miss, presents a whole variety of problems, not least what purpose it was meant to serve: it is far from obvious that its shape suits the Roman liturgy. It has been suggested that it was simply intended as a shrine to St Stephen, the deacon whose martyrdom was recorded in the Acts of the Apostles. This may account for its several doors through which pilgrims might enter, though these were almost immediately blocked up. It probably dates from the pontificate of Pope St Leo the Great (440–61). It was built upon a barracks which housed a special troop of soldiers used for law enforcement within the city and other civic tasks, and also upon a Mithraeum, which may have been a deliberate act.

The saints commemorated here are SS Primus and Felician, two elderly brothers who were executed at the beginning of the fourth century. Their relics were brought here by Pope Theodore I (642–49), who commissioned their chapel to the left of the entrance. A seventh-century mosaic in the apse depicts them. Their relics seem to have been the first to be transferred from outside the walls to a church within the city. The church is dedicated, as has been noted, to St Stephen the protomartyr, but also to St Stephen, King of Hungary (c. 975–1038), who both established Hungary as a kingdom and ensured that it would be Christian by founding dioceses and monasteries. The connection with Hungary began when a religious order founded in Hungary was put in charge. When the Jesuits attempted to establish a Hungarian college for the training of clergy they based it on Santo Stefano, though it did not last and was amalgamated with the German college. However, when Pius VI (1775–95) had the Hungarian church near St Peter's demolished to make way for a sacristy, he added the Hungarian chapel to Santo Stefano, and added the dedication to St Stephen of Hungary. Irish visitors might like to know that King Donough O'Brien of Cashel and Thomond, son of Brian Boru, is buried in the church. He died in Rome in 1064. There is also in the church a medieval episcopal chair, claimed to have been that used by Pope St Gregory I (590–604): the chair is, however, probably no earlier than the thirteenth century.
*Via di Santo Stefano Rotondo 7*

# *Santa Susanna (St Susanna)

The Roman Martyrology commemorates Susanna together with Tiburtius on 11 August. Tiburtius is a bona fide martyr for whom Pope Damasus (366–84) wrote an epitaph. Susanna is much more problematic. The sixth-century legend claims she was the niece of Pope Caius (or Gaius, 283–96) and her father, or perhaps her brother, was called Gabinus: they were put to death at the same time when Susanna refused to marry Diocletian's son. The modern Martyrology says nothing of this, simply that she has long been celebrated as a martyr, but an ancient one says that she died 'at two houses' near the baths of Diocletian. This earlier account is interesting because excavations beneath the church of Santa Susanna revealed a third-century house in such a manner as to suggest that the first church was built more or less exactly on top of it. It is entirely speculative, but it would be nice to think that Susanna – martyr or not – was the owner of the house and subsequently gave her name, the 'titulus', to the church.

It is likely that there was a church here in the fourth century, and it is known that it was rebuilt at the end of the ninth or beginning of the tenth century. It was again rebuilt at the end of the sixteenth and beginning of the seventeenth centuries, and this is the church that survives. It is the national church for citizens of the United States, and it is fitting that it is served by the New York-founded Missionary Society of St Paul the Apostle, or the Paulist Fathers. The relics of a number of saints – though not of St Susanna – are to be found in the chapel of St Lawrence. There are the remains of Genesius the Comedian (for whom, see **San Giovanni della Pigna**) and of Pope St Eleutherius (c. 174–89), as well as, under the altar, the remains of St Felicity of Rome and one of her seven sons. At least, that they were seven sons is the tradition, but it is more likely that they were seven martyrs who were celebrated together and somehow linked to Felicity. She at least still has a feast day listed in the Roman Martyrology: the 'seven sons' do not. Susanna, though not honoured in her relics, is celebrated in much of the iconography of the church, and Gabinus also gets a mention. *Via XX Settembre 14 (Piazza San Bernardo)*

## Santissima Trinità dei Monti
(The Most Holy Trinity of the Hills)

After the view of the dome of St Peter's, the sight of Trinità dei Monti at the top of the Spanish Steps is perhaps the vista most redolent of Rome. The church building itself is pretty uninteresting, but has an interesting history. When King Louis XI of France lay dying he asked for the ministrations of Francis di Paola (1416–1507), a hermit from Calabria, originally a Franciscan but who had founded his own religious order of friars known as the Minims, who received papal approval in 1474. Francis went to the French court reluctantly, but never returned home, dying in Tours and being canonized in 1519. As a form of thanksgiving, Louis XI's successor, Charles VIII, whom the saint had also served as a spiritual guide, bought a vineyard on Rome's Pincian hill and ordered the construction there not only of the church but of a convent for the Minims next door to it. The construction of the church began in 1514 – that of the convent in 1502 – but the church was not consecrated until 1583. It is the French national church in the city. The convent was suppressed in 1797 in the aftermath of the conquest of Rome by Napoleon. The church suffered badly during the occupation, but was refurbished by King Louis XVIII after the restoration of the French monarchy.

There being no more French Minims, the convent was

handed over to St Madeleine Sophie Barat (1779–1865), founder in 1800 of the Society of the Sacred Heart, a religious order devoted to teaching, which received papal approval in 1826. The convent therefore became a school, and now houses a new religious order called the Monastic Fraternities of Jerusalem, founded in 1975. In a chapel in the convent is a picture of the Madonna to which there is considerable devotion, painted in 1844 by a French woman who had been at school there, and who later became a member of the Society of the Sacred Heart. The title of the painting is 'Mater Admirabilis' because, it is claimed, these were the words used by Pius IX on first seeing the picture. Thérèse of Lisieux, St Teresa of the Child Jesus, prayed before the picture when seeking papal permission to enter the Carmelite Order when only 15, a permission which she received. Note, this is in the convent, not the church, and visitors have to ring the bell to gain access. *Piazza della Trinità dei Monti*

## Santuario della Madonna del Divino Amore
(Sanctuary [Shrine] of Our Lady of Divine Love)

This is some way outside Rome – you can take either the 702 bus or the 044 from the Laurentina terminus of the Metro – and it was originally a farm. In 1570 an icon of Our Lady was hung over the gate that led to the farm, and it remained there until 1740. In that year someone was attacked by dogs just outside the farm gate, and appealed to Our Lady for help. The dogs gave up their chase and the story attracted attention, and other miracles were reported as crowds made their way to the spot. The icon was removed temporarily while a chapel was built to house it: it was moved there in 1745. In the early years of the twentieth century the chapel became the centre of a parish, and in the 1930s an enterprising parish priest founded a religious congregation, the Daughters of Our Lady of Divine Love, to help him look after the popular shrine. During World War II the icon (perhaps from the fourteenth century) was brought into Rome and installed in the church of **Sant'Ignazio**: Pope Pius XII and many others came to pray in front of the image for the safety of Rome: the fact that the Allied powers took over the city relatively peacefully was attributed to Our Lady of Divine Love, with the result that devotion to this image increased. It was reinstalled in the original chapel, but another, much larger, church was built to accommodate the crowds that came to venerate the image. In the crypt of the old church are the tombs of the Blessed Luigi Beltrame Quattrocchi (1880–1951) and the Blessed Maria Corsini Beltrame Quattrocchi (1884–1965). They were a married couple (Luigi's second surname is that of the couple who adopted him), and very devout, greatly involved in the Catholic organizations of their day. Of their four children, two became priests and one a nun. They were beatified together in 2001.

## San Tommaso in Formis
(St Thomas [the Apostle] at the Archway)

The archway that gives this small church its name was originally a gateway through Rome's wall but it later became part of an aqueduct carrying water to Nero's palace. The church's origins are obscure, but in 1209 it was handed over to St John of Matha (1160–1213), one of the founders of the Order of the Most Holy Trinity for the Redemption of Captives, a name commonly shortened to Trinitarians. A house was built for members of the order, and a hospice for pilgrims and others in need of accommodation. St John died here, and was interred in the church, but his body was later taken to Spain when the Trinitarians withdrew, although they returned definitively at the end of the nineteenth century. The Trinitarian house had extended over the arch, and St John's cell was converted into a chapel. Part of a finger of the saint is enshrined in the altar. The entrance to the hospice – largely in ruins – has a mosaic showing not only the Trinitarians' symbol but also Christ between two freed slaves, one of whom is white, the other black. This mosaic is dated: it was created in 1218. *Via di San Paolo della Croce 10*


## Transito di Santa Caterina da Siena
(The Passing of St Catherine of Siena)

This is a small chapel in the house which the mystic Catherine of Siena (1347–80) occupied with a group of her disciples from shortly after the time when she came to Rome in 1378 until her death: the chapel is the room in which she died. After a troubled history, it is now cared for by the International Centre for the Study of St Catherine, which once again uses it as a chapel. The saint's body – she was a member of the Dominican Order – has been enshrined in **Santa Maria sopra Minerva**. *Piazza di Santa Chiara*


## Santi Vincenzo e Anastasio a Fontana di Trevi
(SS Vincent [of Saragossa] and Anastasius
[the Persian] at the Trevi Fountain)

The medieval church, dating from at least the tenth century, was completely rebuilt in 1640 at the behest of the French Cardinal Jules Mazarin. It is an attractive baroque building, though unless the pilgrim has a particular, indeed peculiar, interest in the papacy there is no special reason to visit it.

What has been kept here are the internal organs of popes, removed when their bodies were embalmed, from Sixtus V (1585–90) to Leo XIII (1878–1903). These 'praecordia', as they were called, are preserved in jars in the apse. They were kept in this church because the Quirinal Palace, from the late sixteenth century until the fall of Rome in 1870, was the official residence of the popes and lay within the boundaries of this church's parish. Although it remains a Catholic church, and mass is still said once a week, it has been granted to the Bulgarian Orthodox Church as their place of worship in Rome. As the address and indeed the name indicate, it overlooks the famous Trevi Fountain. *Piazza di Trevi*

## Santi Vincenzo e Anastasio alle Tre Fontane
(SS Vincent [of Saragossa] and Anastasius [the Persian] at the Three Springs)

For the story of the beheading of St Paul, see **San Paolo fuori le Mura**. This ancient abbey, now a Cistercian monastery, was erected on the spot where the beheading was supposed to have taken place, though the accounts of this are quite late. The first evidence of an abbey on this site dates from the sixth century, though the present building dates from the latter part of the twelfth and early part of the thirteenth centuries. Though its claim to be the place of St Paul's martyrdom is disputed, it has nonetheless been a pilgrimage destination, and one that took visitors well beyond the walls of Rome. Relics of Vincent of Saragossa (Vincent the Deacon), who was martyred in 304 and is the protomartyr of Spain, were brought here in the fourteenth century, and it is also supposed to retain the head of St Anastasius the Persian, martyred in Caesarea in 628. A more significant relic, if relic it be, is the column to which

St Paul was said to have been tied before his execution. *Via Acqua Salvie 1*


## *San Vitale in Fovea (St Vitalis)

This minor basilica dates from the very late fourth or early fifth century and is dedicated to a martyred bishop of Ravenna. It has been restored several times in the course of its long history, but the portico (itself restored after it had been removed) is much as it would have been when the church was consecrated in 402. Though there are no relics or monuments of significance in the church, it is mentioned here because it was the church of which the English martyred bishop, St John Fisher (1469–1535), became cardinal priest when he was elevated to the rank of cardinal in May 1535: he was executed almost a month to the day later, on 22 June. *Via Nazionale 197B*


## THE CATACOMBS

Catacombs have already been mentioned several times in the text as burial places of the martyrs. There is, or used to be, a romantic notion of Christians in Rome in the first few centuries hiding underground in these cemeteries. It did not happen. The location of these burial places was perfectly well known to the Roman authorities, so it would have been pointless to try to hide there: for example, Pope St Sixtus II was arrested during a visit to a Christian cemetery (see **San Sisto** above). There were Jewish catacombs as well as Christian ones and the best-known catacomb, that of St Callistus (see **San Callisto** above), was first used by a pagan Roman family as its private tomb. Burials in ancient Rome had to be outside the city walls, and so were conveniently placed beside the main roads, along the Via Appia Antica, for example. Catacombs were not limited to Rome – there are even some in Malta – but Rome has a great many of them, partly because they were easy to construct: the volcanic rock, known as tufa, could easily be cut into. Shafts were driven underground then horizontally, with niches, known as 'loculi', for the bodies which were laid on them not in coffins but in shrouds. When the first shaft was complete, another was often dug underneath, with the result that the earliest burials are on the first level and later burials below them. As has been mentioned in the text above, the relics of the saints were moved from the catacombs in the early Middle Ages because of turmoil in the countryside around Rome, and brought into the city – and from there many were dispersed around Europe.

*A typical picture of the inside of a catacomb, except that this chamber, within the Catacomb of St Callistus, was the burial place of nine popes.*

The catacomb at **San Sebastiano fuori le Mura** was never lost sight of, and the seventh-century *Salzburg Itinerary* describes it in detail. However, apart from that at San Sebastiano, they were for the most part forgotten and an antiquarian interest revived only in the seventeenth century. Not all of those now known are open to the public, and even when they are, one usually has to go on a guided tour because it is easy to get lost in the labyrinthine galleries. Finally, it should be said that some of the catacombs are extremely important for the paleo-Christian art which decorates their walls. On the whole, websites dedicated to the catacombs are disappointing. There is, however, useful practical information to be had on the Vatican's website. It is possible to choose an English-language version: vatican.va/roman_curia/pontifical_commissions/archeo. The following list is of those which, according to the Vatican, are open to the public.

## Catacomb of St Agnes: *see* Sant'Agnese fuori le Mura, *Via Nomentana 349*

## Catacomb of Callistus

Perhaps the most visitor-friendly of the catacombs and the most visited, it is of particular interest because of the 'chapel of the popes' where nine bishops of Rome were buried and five 'tombstones' can still be seen. The nine, all saints, were Pontain, Anterus, Fabian, Lucius, Stephen, Sixtus II, Dionysius, Felix and Eutychian. In another part of the catacomb were interred four popes: SS Cornelius (251–53), even though he died in exile in Civitavecchia, Miltiades (311–14), Gaius (283–96) and Eusebius (309). It is believed that a number of bishops of other sees were also interred here. It is here, too, that St Cecilia was placed after her death (cf. **Santa Cecilia in Trastevere** above). In one of the cubicula or rooms within the catacomb there is a third-century painting representing baptism, and another of the Last Supper, among the very earliest examples of Christian art. For a brief life of the Pope after whom the catacomb is named, see **San Callisto**. It is being cared for by the Salesians of Don Bosco. *Via Appia Antica 110*

*A long passageway within the Catacomb of Domitilla: bodies of the deceased were laid in these niches.*

## Catacomb of Domitilla

This catacomb is a series of separate rooms, which at some point were all joined together. It is in the charge of the Divine Word Fathers. *Via delle Sette Chiese 282*

## Catacomb of Marcellinus and Peter: *see* Santi Marcellino e Pietro, *Via Casilina 641*

## Catacomb of Priscilla

Possibly originally intended for the burial place of a patrician Roman family, and named after a member of that family (some commentators think she is depicted in a series of paintings that show a wedding, what may be a nursing mother and a woman at prayer), this is the most richly decorated of the catacombs, painted in the early or mid-third century before the language of Christian art had been developed. Thus an image of Christ as the Good Shepherd depicts him clean-shaven, surrounded by goats, and with a goat, rather than a lamb, over his shoulders. There is also a painting of what seems to be a eucharistic meal, and one of the Madonna and Child – the earliest example of a painting of Mary. There are many more images, from both the Old Testament and the New. A number of martyrs were buried here (see **Santa Prassede**). Also found here was a body which came to be identified as that of St Philomena: her relics were moved to the church of Our Lady of Grace at Mugnano del Cardinale, but the identification has since been disputed and Philomena's feast day is no longer recorded in the Roman Martyrology, though it continues to be celebrated at her shrine. *Via Salaria 430*

## Catacomb of St Sebastian: *see* **San Sebastiano fuori le Mura**, *Via Appia Antica 136*

# MEMENTOS OF CHRIST

The Crown of Thorns *see* Santa Prassede; Santa Croce in Gerusalemme

The Crucifix *see* San Marcello al Corso; La Maddalena; Santa Croce in Gerusalemme

Footprint *see* San Sebastiano fuori le Mura

The Lance *see* San Pietro in Vaticano (St Peter's)

The Mandylion *see* San Silvestro in Capite

A Nail from the Crucifixion *see* Santa Croce in Gerusalemme

The Nativity *see* Santa Maria Maggiore

The Passion *see* Santa Croce in Gerusalemme; San Lorenzo in Lucina

The Pillar of the Scourging *see* Santa Prassede; Santa Croce in Gerusalemme

The Scala Sancta *see* San Giovanni in Laterano

The Seamless Robe *see* Santa Prassede

Stations of the Cross *see* San Bonaventura al Palatino

The Titulus *see* Santa Croce in Gerusalemme

The True Cross *see* San Pietro in Vaticano (St Peter's); San Marcello al Corso; Santa Croce in Gerusalemme

Veronica's Veil *see* San Pietro in Vaticano (St Peter's)

## Images of the Madonna

Madonna dei Monti *see* Santa Maria ai Monti

Madonna del Parto (Our Lady of Childbirth) *see* Sant'Agostino

Madonna della Catena *see* San Silvestro al Quirinale

Madonna della Salute *see* Santa Prassede

Madonna of Divine Love *see* Santuario della Madonna del Divino Amore

Madonna of St Luke *see* Santa Maria del Rosario a Monte Mario

Madonna of the Milk *see* Santa Maria degli Angeli
Madonna of Pilgrims *see* Sant'Agostino
Mater Admirabilis *see* Santissima Trinità dei Monti
Mary, Cause of Our Joy *see* Santa Maria dell'Archetto
Our Lady Health of the Sick *see* La Maddalena
Our Lady Help of Christians (Bon Secours) *see* San Pietro
in Vaticano (St Peter's)
Our Lady of Consolation *see* Santa Maria della
Consolazione
Our Lady of Intercession *see* Sant'Alessio all'Aventino
Our Lady of Graces *see* San Rocco; San Marcello al
Corso; Santa Maria della Consolazione
Our Lady of Guadalupe *see* San Nicola in Carcere
Our Lady of Light *see* Santa Maria della Luce
Our Lady of Mercy *see* Santa Maria in Trastevere
Our Lady of Miracles *see* Santa Maria dei Miracoli
Our Lady of Montesanto *see* Santa Maria in Montesanto
Our Lady of Mount Carmel *see* Sant'Agata in Trastevere;
Santa Maria in Traspontina
Our Lady of Perpetual Succour *see* Sant'Alfonso
de'Liguori all'Esquilino
Our Lady of Piety *see* Santi Bartolomeo ed Alessandro dei
Bergamaschi
Our Lady of Pompeii *see* San Nicola in Carcere
Our Lady of Providence *see* San Carlo ai Catinari
Our Lady Queen of the Apostles *see* Sant'Apollinare
Our Lady of Sorrows *see* San Marcello al Corso
Our Lady of Tears *see* Santa Maria del Pianto
Our Lady of the Column *see* San Pietro in Vaticano (St
Peter's)
Our Lady of the Stairs *see* Santa Maria della Scala
Our Lady of the Street called Cupa *see* Santa Maria in
Trastevere
Our Lady of the Well *see* Santa Maria in Via
Our Lady of Vallicelli *see* Chiesa Nuova

Our Lady of Victory *see* Santa Maria della Vittoria
Our Lady Stairway to Heaven *see* Santa Maria Scala Coeli
Our Lady the Advocate *see* Santa Maria in Via Lata
Our Lady 'Virgo Potens' *see* San Salvatore in Onda
Salus Populi Romani *see* Santa Maria Maggiore
Santa Maria in Portico *see* Santa Maria in Campitelli;
   Santa Maria della Consolazione
Santa Maria Antiqua *see* Santa Francesca Romana
Santissimo Nome di Maria *see* Santissimo Nome di Maria
   al Foro Traiano
*See also* Sant'Andrea delle Fratte

# RELICS OR MEMORIALS OF THE SAINTS

Abundius and Companions *see* Basilica of St
   Bartholomew
Adria *see* Sant'Agata dei Goti
Agapitus *see* Santa Maria in Via Lata
Agnes *see* Sant'Agnese in Agone; Sant'Agnese fuori le
   Mura
Alexander *see* Santa Sabina
Alexis *see* Sant'Alessio all'Aventino
Aloysius Gonzaga *see* Sant'Ignazio
Ambrose *see* Santa Maria degli Angeli
Anastasia *see* San Crisogono
Anastasius the Persian *see* Santi Vincenzo e Anastasio alle
   Tre Fontane
Andrew *see* San Pietro in Vaticano (St Peter's)
Anna Maria Taiga *see* San Crisogono
Anne *see* Sant'Agostino
Augustine of Hippo *see* Sant'Agostino; Santa Maria degli
   Angeli
Balbina, Quirinus and Felicissimus *see* Santa Balbina
   Vergine

Bartholomew *see* San Bartolomeo

Benedict *see* San Benedetto in Piscinula

Benedict Joseph Labre *see* Santa Maria ai Monti; San Martino ai Monti

Bernard of Clairvaux *see* Santa Maria Scala Coeli

Blaise *see* San Biagio della Pagnotta

Bonaventure of Barcelona *see* San Bonaventura al Palatino

Boniface *see* Sant'Alessio all'Aventino

Bridget of Sweden *see* Santa Maria in Monticelli; Santa Prassede; San Paolo fuori le Mura; San Lorenzo in Panisperna

Calepodius *see* Santa Maria in Trastevere

Callistus *see* Santa Maria in Trastevere; San Callisto

Camillus de Lellis *see* La Maddalena

Candida *see* Santa Maria dei Miracoli

Canute *see* Santa Maria in Traspontina

Catherine of Siena *see* Santa Maria sopra Minerva; Transito di Santa Caterina da Siena

Cecilia *see* Santa Cecilia in Trastevere

Charles Borromeo *see* San Carlo ai Catinari; San Carlo al Corso; Santa Prassede

Charles of Sezze *see* San Francesco d'Assisi a Ripa Grande

Chrysogonus *see* San Crisogono

Constance *see* Santa Costanza

Cornelius *see* Santa Maria in Trastevere

Cosmas *see* Santi Cosma e Damiano

Crispin and Crispinian *see* San Lorenzo in Panisperna

Crispus, Crispianus and Benedicta *see* Santi Giovanni e Paolo

Cyriac *see* Santa Maria degli Angeli

Cyril (and Methodius) *see* San Clemente

Damasus *see* San Lorenzo in Damaso

Damian *see* Santi Cosma e Damiano

Degna *see* San Marcello al Corso

Dionysius *see* San Silvestro in Capite

Dominic *see* Santa Sabina; San Sisto Vecchio; Santa Maria
    del Rosario a Monte Mario
Dominic Barberi *see* Santi Giovanni e Paolo
Domitilla *see* Santi Nereo e Achilleo; Chiesa Nuova
Dorothy *see* Santa Dorotea
Eleutherius *see* Santa Susanna
Elizabeth Canori Mora *see* San Carlo alle Quattro Fontane
Elizabeth Sanna *see* San Salvatore in Onda
Emerentiana *see* Sant'Agnese fuori le Mura
Eusebius of Bologna *see* Sant'Eusebio all'Esquilino
Eustace *see* Santa Maria in Monticelli
Eventius *see* Santa Sabina
Expeditus *see* Santa Maria di Loreto
Fabian *see* San Sebastiano fuori le Mura
Felicity *see* Santa Susanna
Felix of Cantalice *see* Santa Maria della Concezione;
    Santa Croce e San Bonaventura dei Lucchesi
Fra Angelico *see* Santa Maria sopra Minerva
Frances of Rome *see* Sant'Agnese in Agone; Santa
    Francesca Romana
Francis Caracciola *see* Sant'Angelo in Pescheria
Francis di Paola *see* Trinità dei Monti
Francis of Assisi *see* San Francesco d'Assisi a Ripa Grande
Francis Xavier *see* the Gesù; Sant'Andrea al Quirinale;
    San Francesco Saverio del Caravita
Gaspare del Bufalo *see* Santa Maria in Trivio
Genesius [the Comedian] *see* San Giovanni della Pigna;
    Santa Susanna
George *see* San Giorgio in Velabro
Giuseppe Maria Tomasi *see* Sant'Andrea della Valle; San
    Martin ai Monti
Gregory of Nazianzen *see* Santa Maria in Campitelli
Gregory the Great *see* Santa Croce in Gerusalemme; Santo
    Stefano Rotondo; San Pietro in Vaticano (St Peter's);
    Santa Maria degli Angeli

Helena *see* Santa Maria in Aracoeli; Santa Croce in
 Gerusalemme; San Pietro in Vaticano (St Peter's)
Hippolytus *see* Sant'Agata dei Goti
Hyacinthe-Marie Cormier s*ee* Santi Domenico e Sisto
Ignatius of Antioch *see* San Clemente
Ignatius Loyola *see* the Gesù; San Paolo fuori le Mura;
 San Pietro in Montorio
Jerome *see* Santa Maria Maggiore; San Pietro in Vaticano
 (St Peter's); Santa Maria degli Angeli; San Girolamo
 della Carità; Sant'Anastasia
John and Paul *see* Santi Giovanni e Paolo
John the Evangelist *see* San Giovanni a Porta Latina
John Baptist de Rossi *see* Santa Maria in Cosmedin
John Berchmans *see* Sant'Ignazio
John Chrysostom *see* San Pietro in Vaticano (St Peter's)
John Fisher *see* San Vitale in Fovea
John Henry Newman *see* Santi Giovanni e Paolo; San
 Giorgio in Velabro
John Kalibytes *see* San Giovanni Calibita
John Leonardi *see* Santa Maria in Campitelli
John of Matha *see* San Tommaso in Formis
John XXIII *see* San Pietro in Vaticano (St Peter's); Santi
 Bartolomeo ed Alessandro dei Bergamaschi
John Paul II *see* San Pietro in Vaticano (St Peter's)
Josaphat *see* San Pietro in Vaticano (St Peter's)
Joseph *see* Sant'Anastasia
Joseph Calasanz (Calasanctius) *see* San Pantaleo
Justin Martyr *see* Santa Maria della Concezione
Largus *see* Santa Maria degli Angeli
Lawrence *see* San Lorenzo in Lucina; San Lorenzo fuori le
 Mura; San Lorenzo in Panisperna
Leo I the Great *see* San Pietro in Vaticano (St Peter's)
Leo II *see* San Pietro in Vaticano (St Peter's)
Leo III *see* San Pietro in Vaticano (St Peter's)
Leonard of Port Maurice *see* San Bonaventura al Palatino

Leontia *see* San Francesco d'Assisi a Ripa Grande

Lucius I *see* Santa Cecilia in Trastevere

Ludovica Albertoni *see* San Francesco d'Assisi a Ripa Grande

Luigi Beltrame Quattrocchi and Maria Corsini Beltrame Quattrocchi *see* Santuario della Madonna del Divino Amore

Madeleine Sophie Barat *see* Santissima Trinità dei Monti

Marcellina *see* Sant'Ambrogio della Massima

Marcellinus (Pope) *see* Santa Maria degli Angeli

Marcellinus (priest) *see* Santi Marcellino e Pietro

Marcellus *see* San Marcello al Corso

Marcia *see* Martia

Margaret of Cortona *see* Santa Balbina Vergine

Mark and Marcellian *see* San Nicola in Carcere

Martia *see* Sant'Agata dei Goti; Santi Marcellino e Pietro

Martin I *see* San Martino ai Monti

Martina *see* Santi Luca e Martina

Mary *see* Sant'Anastasia

Mary of Jesus *see* Santa Croce e San Bonaventura dei Lucchesi

Matthew *see* San Luigi dei Francesi

Matthias *see* Santa Maria Maggiore

Maximilian *see* Santa Maria in Monticelli

Maximilian Kolbe *see* Sant'Andrea delle Fratte

Maximus *see* Santa Cecilia in Trastevere

Maximus the Centurion *see* Santa Maria degli Angeli

Merita *see* San Marcello al Corso

Michael Garicoïts *see* Santa Maria dei Miracoli

Monica *see* Sant'Agostino

Neon *see* Sant'Agata dei Goti

Nereus and Achilleus *see* Santi Nereo e Achilleo; Chiesa Nuova

Nicholas of Myra *see* San Saba

Nicola Saggio *see* San Francesco di Paola ai Monti

Nympha *see* Santa Maria in Monticelli

Oliver Plunkett *see* San Girolamo della Carità

Paul *see* San Paolo alla Regola; San Giovanni in Laterano; San Paolo fuori le Mura; Santa Maria in Traspontina; Santa Maria in Via Lata; Santi Vincenzo e Anastasio alle Tre Fontane; San Paolo alle Tre Fontane; Santa Maria Scala Coeli

Paul VI *see* San Pietro in Vaticano (St Peter's)

Paula *see* San Girolamo della Carità

Paulinus of Nola *see* Basilica of St Bartholomew

Peter *see* San Giovanni in Laterano; Santa Pudenziana; Santa Francesca Romana; San Pietro in Vincoli; Santa Prisca; Santa Maria in Traspontina; Santa Maria in Via Lata; San Giuseppe dei Falegnami; San Pietro in Montorio

Peter (2) *see* Santi Marcellino e Pietro

Philip Neri *see* San Giovanni Battista dei Fiorentini; Chiesa Nuova; San Girolamo della Carità

Philomena *see* Catacomb of Priscilla

Pius V *see* Santa Maria Maggiore; Santa Sabina

Pius IX *see* San Lorenzo fuori le Mura

Pius X *see* Santa Prassede; San Pietro in Vaticano (St Peter's)

Polycarp *see* Sant'Ambrogio della Massima

Praxedes *see* Santa Prassede

Primus and Felician *see* Santo Stefano Rotondo

Prisca *see* Santa Prisca

Pudens *see* San Giovanni in Laterano; Santa Pudenziana

Pudentiana *see* Santa Prassede

Quirinus *see* San Sebastiano fuori le Mura

Quodvultdeus *see* Santa Maria in Monticelli

Robert Bellarmine *see* Sant'Ignazio; Santa Maria in Via

Sabas *see* San Saba

Sebastian *see* San Sebastiano fuori le Mura

Servulus *see* San Clemente

Smaragdus *see* Santa Maria degli Angeli

Simplicianus, Faustus and Beatrice *see* San Nicola in Carcere

Sixtus *see* San Sisto Vecchio

Stanislaus Kostka *see* Sant'Andrea al Quirinale

Stephen *see* San Lorenzo fuori le Mura

Stephen (Pope) *see* San Silvestro in Capite

Sylvester *see* San Silvestro in Capite

Sylvia *see* San Saba

Xystus *see* Sixtus

Tarcisius *see* San Silvestro in Capite

Teresa of Avila *see* Santa Maria della Vittoria; Santa Maria della Scala

Teresa of the Child Jesus *see* Thérèse of Lisieux

Theodolus *see* Santa Sabina

Thérèse of Lisieux *see* Santissima Trinità dei Monti

Thomas Aquinas

Thomas of Canterbury (Thomas Becket) *see* Santa Maria Maggiore; Sant'Alessio all'Aventino

Thomas the Apostle *see* Santa Croce in Gerusalemme

Tiburtius *see* Santa Cecilia in Trastevere

Turibius *see* Sant'Anastasia

Urban I *see* Santa Maria in Trastevere; Santa Cecilia in Trastevere

Valentine *see* Santa Maria in Cosmedin

Valerian *see* Santa Cecilia in Trastevere

Victoria *see* San Lorenzo in Panisperna

Vincent of Saragossa (Vincent the Deacon) *see* Santi Vincenzo e Anastasio alle Tre Fontane

Vincent Pallotti *see* San Salvatore in Onda

Vittoria *see* Santa Maria in Campitelli

Xystus *see* Sixtus

Zeno *see* Santa Prassede

# The National Colleges

Because it was impossible during the Penal Days to educate those wishing to be priests in the British Isles, colleges were founded in Rome and elsewhere (there is still an English college in Valladolid, for example). They are more like residences, providing spiritual formation to their students, than colleges: the teaching of philosophy and theology generally speaking takes place elsewhere, in the Roman universities such as the Gregorianum, run by the Society of Jesus, or the Angelicum, in the charge of the Order of Preachers – the Dominicans. There are several others run by different religious orders, and the Lateran run by diocesan clergy. In addition there are a number of specialized institutes such as the Biblicum and the Orientale, both run by Jesuits, where higher courses can be taken in Scripture and the Eastern churches.

## Beda

The Beda College (its patron saint is the Venerable Bede) was founded in 1852 to accommodate British converts to Roman Catholicism, often themselves already clergymen, who wished to study for the priesthood in communion with Rome. It is an exception to the note above because teaching is very largely provided in-house. Those coming to the college were usually older men for whom the standard six- or seven-year university course was unsuitable, and were in any case uncomfortable with the regime imposed upon younger men normally coming, at that time, straight from school. It was therefore predominantly a college for what were called 'late vocations', and so it has remained although the students now come from all over the world. It remains, however, under the aegis of the

Bishops' Conference of England and Wales. The language of instruction, unlike many of the other Roman teaching institutions, is English. In 1960 the college moved to a site – Vatican property – right next door to **San Paolo fuori le Mura**. *Pontificio Collegio Beda, Viale San Paolo 18, 00146 Roma* (+39 06551271)

## English

The remote history of the Venerable English College, often simply referred to as the Venerabile, goes back to the English settlement in Rome (cf. **Santo Spirito in Sassia**). The hospice welcoming English pilgrims to Rome began on the present site, however, in the 1360s and 1370s: a house on Via di Monserrato was bought by a layman in 1361. There were a number of famous guests including, as a brochure of the college says, 'the excitable mystic Margery Kemp'. Even Thomas Cromwell came to visit. It was not then a college. It began as such in 1579, well after the religious break between Rome and England, in order to train priests for the mission in England: the students took the 'missionary oath' to return to their homeland, and many died there a martyr's death. Though for a few years it was in the charge of diocesan clergy – not that there were any longer dioceses – for most of its existence until the suppression of the Society of Jesus in 1773 it was run by Jesuits. After the suppression it was once again run by secular clergy. The students at one time could not return home, even in the summer, and they used to take a vacation at a 'villa house'. From 1920 the villa house has been at Palazzola in the Alban Hills, and it is now much in demand as accommodation for pilgrimages as well as conferences, weddings and straightforward holidays. Further details can be found via the Venerabile's website. *Venerabile Collegio Inglese,*

*Via di Monserrato 45, 00186 Roma* (+39 066868546 or +39 066865808)

## Irish

The learned Irish Franciscan, Fr Luke Wadding, founded the Irish College in 1628, and it remained in the charge of Franciscans for the first part of its life. In 1635, however, it was handed over to the Jesuits who governed it for over a century with the help of Irish secular clergy. When it was re-established after the Napoleonic wars its original home on the Via degli Ibernesi had been taken over by nuns, and the college moved to a site beside **Sant'Agata dei Goti**, then, in 1926, to its present site not far from **San Giovanni in Laterano**. The college not only makes a point of advertising its hospitality to visitors during the summer months, it now also offers accommodation throughout the year. *Via dei Santi Quattro 1, 00184 Roma* (+39 06772631; reception@ irishcollege.org; ufficio@irishcollege.org [apparently for those looking for accommodation]; and – self-explanatory – weddings@irishcollege.org, for which there is a separate telephone number: +39 0677263501)

## Scots

The college was founded in December 1600, and in 1604 settled into its long-time residence on the Via delle Quattro Fontane in central Rome. There it stayed until 1962 when it moved to its present site just north of the city. From 1615 until 1773, when the Society of Jesus was suppressed by order of Pope Clement XIV, it was in the charge of Jesuits. For most of the time from then on it has been run by clergy from Scotland. *Pontificio Collegio Scozzese, Via*

*Cassia 481, 00189 Roma* (+39 063366801; email: office@ scotscollege.it)

## North American

The suggestion that there might be a North American college was made in 1854, not by a prelate from the USA but by Cardinal Nicholas Wiseman, the recently appointed (1850) archbishop of Westminster. North America was still considered to be mission territory, and so responsibility for setting up the college fell to the Congregation for the Propagation of the Faith, which acquired a property in the Via dell'Umiltà. Staff and students moved there in December 1859 – they had previously studied at the Collegium Urbanum run by the Congregation. Like the other English-speaking Roman colleges, the Americans had to move out during World War II: soon after they returned it became obvious that it was too small for the numbers wishing to study in Rome. In October 1953, therefore, the college moved to a new building on the Janiculum, constructed to hold three hundred seminarians. There is no suggestion on their website that visitors to Rome can stay in the college, but it supports an excellent Visitors' Centre at Via dell'Umiltà 30 (+39 0669001821/2; visitorsoffice@ pnac.org), though it is clear that it chiefly serves people from across the Atlantic. The office's website, however, contains a great many useful links, including suggestions for places to stay. The college itself seems shy of visitors. The mailing address on its website appears to be a post box within the Vatican City. The street address is: *Pontifical North American College (PNAC), Via del Gianicolo 14, 00165 Roma* (+39 06684931)

# Glossary

**Basilica**: The term basilica is derived from the Greek for king ('basileus') and was a hall meant for large gatherings, for the meetings of law courts for example. By the early fourth century the architectural form of such halls was of a building with a wide central nave, to use the ecclesiastical term, and at least two side aisles, with a clerestory above allowing in light, and an apse at one (usually the east) end. The form of these state edifices was easily adapted for use as churches. Unlike the state ones, however, the Christian basilicas were highly decorated on the inside, and resplendent with gold and silver ornaments such as candlesticks. The term is also used of certain important churches outside Rome which can be of various architectural styles. As an honorific title, 'basilica' is conferred by papal decree, and the church then enjoys certain privileges such as the right to display the papal coat of arms over the door and to grant particular indulgences to those who visit them.

**Indulgences**: A Catholic can perform certain actions, say certain prayers or visit certain places to gain an indulgence, which is the remission of the punishment incurred by sin: a plenary indulgence is the remission of all punishment that a sinner has incurred. The punishment was a form of penance imposed by the Church through the bishop or priest on a person who had committed a sin. He or she was, for instance, required to say certain prayers (still the common practice) or fast for a certain number of days, or go on pilgrimage. Penitentiaries, books listing the 'tariffs' of penance for sins, came from Ireland into Britain and then spread to continental Europe. The notion of an exact tariff was dying out by the Middle Ages, but the practice had developed of commuting these tariffs, of a certain number of days of penance, or all of them, into an 'indulgence' which might even be 'bought', though this was technically an example of almsgiving. It was of course against this trade in indulgences that Martin Luther revolted. The Reformation did not, however, put an end to indulgences within Catholicism: indeed, perhaps as a reaction they multiplied, though the simoniacal act of buying them disappeared. Indulgences have largely died out, though they are still listed and can be encountered at shrines, on prayer cards and elsewhere. Though few people nowadays may set out to journey to Rome or Compostela or Jerusalem – or in England to Walsingham or Canterbury, for example – specifically to gain an indulgence, they were for many a motivating force for pilgrimage during the Middle Ages.

**The Seven Churches**: Very early on in the history of pilgrimage to Rome seven churches were given prominence as those that had to be visited, largely because of their connection with the martyrs. These are all described above, but for convenience they are listed here: San Pietro in Vaticano (St Peter's); San Paolo fuori le Mura (St Paul's Outside the Walls); San Giovanni in Laterano (St John Lateran); Santa Maria Maggiore (St Mary Major); Santa Croce in Gerusalemme (The Holy Cross in Jerusalem); San Lorenzo fuori le Mura (St Lawrence Outside the Walls); San Sebastiano fuori le Mura (St Sebastian Outside the Walls).

**The Seven Hills**: A number of cities claim to have been built on seven hills, but Rome is the best known of them. The hills are important, because directions are often given using their names, 'on the Janiculum' or 'on the Aventine'. In fact the enumeration of the original seven would not include the Janiculum, nor indeed the Vatican hill on which St Peter's was built, because they lay on the west bank of the River Tiber, outside the city walls. The traditional seven are the Quirinal, on which is a former papal palace, now the residence of Italy's president, the Esquiline, the Aventine, the Capitoline, the Palatine, the Viminal and the Pincian, all of which are on the east bank of the Tiber. Ascending the Aventine and the Janiculum can be quite challenging on a very hot day, as can climbing the steps to the Capitol, but for the most part the hills of Rome are fairly gentle slopes, sometimes so gentle one would hardly notice the incline.

**Stational churches:** The Christian origin of the term 'statio' is unclear, though it may have been used first for days of fasting, which the early Christians did on Wednesdays and Fridays, and then for the places where the Eucharist was celebrated, whether in 'tituli' (see below) or at the graves of martyrs, particularly on the anniversaries of their deaths. The Bishop of Rome moved from one 'station' to another on these days, perhaps as a means of uniting the large but diverse communities of Christians in the city. The practice is very old, possibly as old as the end of the second century, but the 'stational churches' system as such is perhaps only as old as the late fifth century when it was associated with the emergence of Lent as a fully fledged liturgical season, by which time all the stational churches had been built in various parts of the city. The bishop travelled to each one of them in turn, and in later times he would have gone in procession, though processions, which came to be associated with the stational churches, developed rather later, being attested only from the late sixth century. They became rather grand affairs with processional crosses, each with three candles attached, a choir ('schola') chanting the litany, military banners held aloft and the relics of saints being carried along. Processions were fairly short – they might take about an hour – and began at places where there was outside the church a convenient piazza on which the worshippers might collect – and where a 'collect' was read. Below is a list of stational churches for Lent. The practice of visiting these has been fostered by the North American College, from whose website the list is taken. Any pilgrim who is in Rome during the Lenten season is welcome to join this devotion: further details can be found on the website at:

www.pnac.org/station-churches/the-roman-station-liturgy/

| Lenten Day | Church |
|---|---|
| Ash Wednesday | S. Sabina all'Aventino |
| Thursday | S. Giorgio al Velabro |
| Friday | SS Giovanni e Paolo |
| Saturday | S. Agostino |
| Sunday – WEEK I | S. Giovanni in Laterano |
| Monday | S. Pietro in Vincoli |
| Tuesday | S. Anastasia al Palatino |
| Wednesday | S. Maria Maggiore |
| Thursday | S. Lorenzo in Panisperna |
| Friday | SS Dodici Apostoli |
| Saturday | S. Pietro in Vaticano |
| Sunday – WEEK II | S. Maria in Domnica |
| Monday | S. Clemente |
| Tuesday | S. Balbina all'Aventino |
| Wednesday | S. Cecilia in Trastevere |
| Thursday | S. Maria in Trastevere |

# GLOSSARY

| Lenten Day | Church |
|---|---|
| Friday | S. Vitale |
| Saturday | SS Pietro e Marcellino |
| Sunday – WEEK III | S. Lorenzo Fuori le Mura |
| Monday | S. Marco al Campidoglio |
| Tuesday | S. Pudenziana al Viminale |
| Wednesday | S. Sisto |
| Thursday | SS Cosma e Damiano |
| Friday | S. Lorenzo in Lucina |
| Saturday | S. Susanna |
| Sunday – WEEK IV | S. Croce in Gerusalemme |
| Monday | SS Quattro Coronati |
| Tuesday | S. Lorenzo in Damaso |
| Wednesday | S. Paolo fuori le Mura |
| Thursday | SS Silvestro e Martino |
| Friday | S. Eusebio all'Esquilino |
| Saturday | S. Nicola in Carcere |
| Sunday – WEEK V | S. Pietro in Vaticano |
| Monday | S. Crisogono in Trastevere |
| Tuesday | S. Maria in Via Lata |
| Wednesday | S. Marcello al Corso |
| Thursday | S. Apollinare |
| Friday | S. Stefano Rotondo |
| Saturday | S. Giovanni a Porta Latina |
| Palm Sunday | S. Giovanni in Laterano |
| Monday | S. Prassede all'Esquilino |
| Tuesday | S. Prisca all'Aventino |
| Wednesday | S. Maria Maggiore |

These churches are marked in the text with an asterisk (*).

**Titular churches:** To understand Christian Rome it is important to remember that during the early Christian era the city's population was in decline. It probably reached its peak of 1.5 million in the second century, but by the time Constantine granted legal recognition to Christianity it had dropped to around 800,000 of whom possibly about a quarter were converts to the new faith. The decline in population which continued into the mid-sixth century, by which time it is thought there were no more than 30,000, meant that there were large open spaces in the centre of Rome, while the people who remained lived on the seven hills – with the richest at the top of the hills – and in Trastevere, the area immediately *trans Tiberim*, across the Tiber, in other words, on the same side of the river as the Vatican. The Christian 'churches' were obviously located in the populated areas, though often discreetly on the edge.

The word 'churches' is in inverted commas, because they were not churches at all but private houses, and the names of the owners of these houses were displayed on a plaque attached to the house. This was called a 'titulus'. Some of these houses were used for Christian worship, and eventually developed into churches, but as private houses would not have been recognized by the general population as Christian centres. Because of these plaques the oldest churches are known as 'tituli' and are scattered around Rome, though three of them (San Crisogono, San Callisto and Santa Cecilia) are close together in Trastevere which seems to have been a focus of early Christianity in the city. By the end of the fourth century 20 'tituli' are recorded: half a century later five more had been added. The first list is drawn from the parishes, if that word can be used, of the priests who signed the Acts of a synod held in Rome in 499. Originally the 'house churches' would have been called after the person whose name was on the 'titulus', the owner in other words, but during the sixth century the owner's name often acquired the appellation 'saint', or the buildings were entirely renamed and given a saint's name. In addition, cardinals by a historical fiction are bishops of the sees around Rome, or priests or deacons of the churches of the city itself. As such they have a 'titular church', one to which they theoretically belong, and this church will display its particular cardinal's coat of arms above the door.

The mention of cardinal deacons raises another issue about the titular churches. Deacons were the men in charge of the Church of Rome's welfare services in the different regions of the city. As such they were often better known, or more popular, than the priests and in the early centuries were frequently elected bishop. They needed a base for their operations, perhaps to store grain and other foodstuffs. Some of the 'tituli' were converted into deaconries. Among the first, at the end of the seventh century and early in the eighth, were San Giorgio in Velabro ('Velabrum' was the name of a Roman street where there was a market for, especially, cheese and oil but also other commodities and was therefore particularly appropriate as a deaconry), Santa Maria in Cosmedin ('Cosmedin' comes from a Greek word meaning 'ornate'), San Teodoro and Santa Maria in Via Lata ('Via Lata' means 'broad street' and was one of the main Roman thoroughfares, now the Corso). The same thing happened in the eighth century under Pope Hadrian I (772–95) to the churches of Santi Sergio e Baccho, Santi Cosma e Damiano and, under Leo III (795–816), to San Martino ai Monti and Santi Nereo ed Achilleo.

# Bibliography

Baldovin, John, *The Urban Character of Christian Worship* (Rome: Oriental Institute, 1987)

Barefoot, Brian, *The English Road to Rome* (Upton-Upon-Severn: Images, 1993)

Champ, Judith, *The English Pilgrimage to Rome* (Leominster: Gracewing, 2000)

Claridge, Amanda, *Rome: An Oxford Archaeological Guide* (Oxford: Oxford University Press, 2010)

Farmer, David, *Oxford Dictionary of Saints* (Oxford: Oxford University Press, 2011)

Hart, Vaughan and Hicks, Peter (editors and translators), *Palladio's Rome* (New Haven: Yale University Press, 2006)

Kelly, J. N. D., revised by M. J. Walsh, *Oxford Dictionary of Popes* (Oxford: Oxford University Press, 2010)

Korn, Frank J., *A Catholic's Guide to Rome* (New York: Paulist Press, 2000)

Luff, S. G. A., *The Christian's Guide to Rome* (Tunbridge Wells: Burns and Oates, 1990)

McGregor, James H. S., *Rome from the Ground Up* (Cambridge, MA: Belknap Press of Harvard University Press, 2005)

*Martyrologium Romanum* (Vatican: Typis Vaticanis, 2004)

Masson, Georgina, revised by John Fort, *The Companion Guide to Rome* (Woodbridge: Companion Guides, 2009)

Nelson, Howard, *The Einsiedeln Itinaries: A Pilgrim's Guide to Rome in Charlemagne's Time* (Hertford: Confraternity of Pilgrims to Rome, 2013)

Nelson, Howard, *Rome: The Early Church: A Pilgrim's Guide* (Hertford: Confraternity of Pilgrims to Rome, 2011)

# BIBLIOGRAPHY

Nichols, Francis Morgan (editor and translator), *The Marvels of Rome/Mirabilia Urbis Romanae* (New York: Italica Press, 1986)

Nickel, Joe, *The Jesus Relics* (Stroud: The History Press, 2008)

Reardon, Wendy J., *The Deaths of the Popes* (Jefferson, NC and London: McFarland, 2004)

*Secret Rome* (Paris: Jonglez, 2010)

Vidon, Henry, *The Pilgrim's Guide to Rome* (London: Sheed and Ward, 1975)

# Index

# INDEX